# 1,000 TRIVIA FACTS ABOUT THE BIBLE

ZONDERVAN®

ZONDERVAN

*1,000 Trivia Facts About the Bible*

Copyright © 2014 by Zondervan

Portions of this book are extracted from *NIV Fast Facts Bible* © 2014, 9780310432166.

Requests for information should be addressed to:
Zondervan, *3900 Sparks Dr. SE, Grand Rapids, Michigan 49546*

Zondervan titles may be purchased in bulk for educational, business, fundraising, or sales promotional use. For information, please email SpecialMarkets@Zondervan.com.

ISBN 978-0-310-15152-4 (softcover)

**Library of Congress Cataloging-in-Publication Data on File**

Scripture quotations marked NIV are taken from The Holy Bible, New International Version®, NIV®. Copyright © 1973, 1978, 1984, 2011 by Biblica, Inc.® Used by permission of Zondervan. All rights reserved worldwide. www.Zondervan.com. The "NIV" and "New International Version" are trademarks registered in the United States Patent and Trademark Office by Biblica, Inc.®

Cover design: Jamie DeBruyn
Interior design: Chris Hudson

*Printed in the United States of America*

23 24 25 26 27 28 29 30 31  / LSC /  12 11 10 9 8 7 6 5 4 3 2 1

**Trivia lovers, rejoice!** Learning the fascinating facts and fun stories about the Bible has never been easier.

Whether used for personal reading, homeschooling, family fun night, or stumping your Sunday school class, *1,000 Trivia Facts About the Bible* will help you learn the Bible in an engaging, enlightening new way.

This book highlights the main themes in each Bible book, including buzzwords, key words, and interesting facts about the book. For example, did you know that the book of Genesis has 50 chapters, 1,522 verses, and more than 38,000 words?

Each book also has a trivia quiz, giving you the opportunity to find out how much you remember from the Bible book. Fun categories like "Hot Seat," "Where in the World," and "Who Dunnit?" provide intriguing quiz questions on the most important parts of each chapter. "Time Traveler" questions help you take a step back in time into the life of a Bible character. You can casually read through the questions in the quizzes to see how much you retained from reading the Bible book or use them as a deeper study guide to help your small group learn more about the Bible.

*1,000 Trivia Facts About the Bible* is designed to help you get to know God's Word better. Spend some time reading through your favorite Bible book, and pay attention to unique and interesting details about the characters, settings, events, and messages in the pages. May your reading experience be greatly enriched as you explore the fascinating details included in your Bible.

# THE **OLD TESTAMENT**

KEY WORDS:
CREATION • SIN • FLOOD • COVENANT • PROMISE

# GENESIS

## NAMES FOR GOD IN GENESIS

**God Most High (El Elyon)** *(14:18,22)*

**Eternal God (El-Olam)** *(21:33)*

**God Almighty (El-Shaddai)** *(17:1)*

**The Lord will Provide (Jehovah-Jireh)** *(22:14)*

## BY THE NUMBERS

**50** CHAPTERS

**1533** VERSES

**38,267** WORDS

## DID YOU KNOW ?

▶ Did you know that according to Jewish tradition, Jacob was 80-years-old when he first laid eyes on Rachel?

▶ Hagar was born in Egypt *(16:1)*

## FATHER OF FAITH?

Though Abraham is known as the father of faith, he wasn't perfect; the Bible lists a number of faults that offer a glimpse into his human frailty.

Asks Sarah to lie and say she is his sister, thereby allowing her to be taken into Pharaoh's harem *(12:11–13)*

Doesn't trust God to provide an heir through Sarah, so he sleeps with her Egyptian slave (Hagar) to produce one *(16:1–4)*

Laughs when God promises he and Sarah will have a son *(17:15–17)*

Again lies and says Sarah is his sister, allowing her to be taken into King Abimelek's harem *(20:1–5)*

# GENESIS IN REVIEW

### HOT SEAT
1. My grandpa is one of the most famous people in Bible history, and my son, Nimrod, became famous as a mighty hunter. Who am I?

### MINUTIAE & MISCELLANY
2. How did Isaac meet his wife Rebekah?

A. Met her shepherding in Ramah

B. Saw her at a well with her water jar

C. Abraham had her brought to him

D. Won her in a poker game

### WHO DUNNIT?
3. King Abimelek of the Philistines caught sight of this man caressing his wife, although he had represented her only as his sister. Who was he?

### WHERE IN THE WORLD
4. Which of these is not one of the four headwaters from Eden?

A. Gihon

B. Habor

C. Euphrates

D. Pishon

### WHO SAID IT?
5. Who uttered this line from a place he called Peniel: "It is because I saw God face to face, and yet my life was spared"?

### TIME TRAVELER
6. You have been banished by God to be a "restless wanderer on the earth," and you have settled in the land of Nod, east of Eden. Who are you?

### WHO DUNNIT?
7. Jacob came to Canaan and bought a piece of ground from Hamor the Hivite, where he pitched his tent. What crime did Hamor's son commit against Jacob's family?

A. Killed Jacob's servant

B. Took Leah's servant girl

C. Raped Jacob's daughter

D. Stole their flocks by night

### HOT SEAT
8. As the sun was setting and I fell into a deep sleep, a thick and dreadful darkness came over me and the Lord spoke to me. Who am I?

### MINUTIAE & MISCELLANY
9. To whom was God speaking when he said, "The fear and dread of you will fall on all the beasts of the earth, and on all the birds in the sky, on every creature that moves along the ground, and on all the fish in the sea; they are given into your hands"?

A. Jacob and Esau

B. Adam and Eve

C. Noah and his sons

D. Ishmael

### TIME TRAVELER
10. You are Abraham's son, and you have many children. Who is your firstborn son?

A. Nebaioth

B. Kedar

C. Adbeel

D. Mibsam

### HOT SEAT
11. It was so confusing! I was carrying a bundle of cut sticks, and Dad had some fire and his trusty knife. We didn't have anything else with us, not even a lamb! Who am I?

### MINUTIAE & MISCELLANY
12. What did Rachel name her youngest son, before his father renamed him Benjamin?

A. Ben-Jih

B. Ben-Oni

C. Obadiah

D. Obi-Wan Kenobi

# EXODUS

## What's In A Name?

Names and Meanings

MARAH = Bitter *(15:23)*

MASSAH = Testing *(17:7)*

MERIBAH = Quarreling *(17:7)*

GERSHOM = Foreigner *(2:22; 18:3)*

ELIEZER = God is my helper *(18:4)*

## WHAT'S YOUR SKILL?

*God Gives Skills to People to Serve Him 35:30–35*

Metalworking with gold, silver, bronze

Cutting and setting stones

Artistic crafting

Engraving

Designing

Embroidering

Weaving

## FACTS IN THE BOX

*Miracles Placed in the Ark of the Covenant Hebrews 9:4*

Jar of manna

Aaron's staff that budded

Stone tablets of the Ten Commandments

## BY THE NUMBERS

40 CHAPTERS

1,213 VERSES

28,524 WORDS

# PROPHECIES

## Sacrificial Lamb of God

## Blood protection

### Salvation from slavery into God's presence

# EXODUS IN REVIEW

### ⏱ TIME TRAVELER

1. You were born in Egypt but eventually led your people out of that terrible place. Your father was of the tribe of Levi. What tribe was your mother from?

A. Judah

B. Reuben

C. Levi

D. Apache

### Q WHO SAID IT?

2. "Because hands were lifted up against the throne of the Lord, the Lord will be at war against the Amalekites from generation to generation."

### 🔥 HOT SEAT

3. I saved some girls from shepherds at the well today. They went home and told their dad, the priest. Do you know who they said I was?

A. An Egyptian

B. An Israelite

C. An Amalekite

D. A Midianite

### Q WHO SAID IT?

4. "So I told them, 'Whoever has any gold jewelry, take it off.' Then they gave me the gold, and I threw it into the fire, and out came this calf!"

### ⬅ THEN VS. NOW

5. Which river, which provides hydroelectric power today, served as an important source of water and other resources for ancient Egypt?

A. Tigris

B. Nile

C. Euphrates

D. Hudson

### Q WHO SAID IT?

6. Who said to Pharaoh, "This is the finger of God"?

A. Pharaoh's daughter

B. Moses and Aaron

C. Pharaoh's magicians

D. Pharaoh's son

### "?" CRYPTIC PHRASES

7. Where were the Urim and Thummim located?

A. West of the Red Sea

B. In Egypt, near the Nile River

C. In Pharaoh's castle dungeon

D. In a priest's breastplate

### Q WHO SAID IT?

8. "What is this you are doing for the people? Why do you alone sit as judge, while all these people stand around you from morning till evening?"

### 🏅 MINUTIAE & MISCELLANY

9. Where did Aaron get the gold to make the golden calf that the Israelites worshipped while Moses was away receiving the law?

### ✗ WHO DUNNIT?

10. What nation attacked the Israelites at Rephidim?

### 🌐 WHERE IN THE WORLD

11. What was the name of the place where the Israelites camped that had 12 springs and 70 palm trees?

### 🔥 HOT SEAT

12. I filled a jar with manna, then placed it with the commandment tablets from the mountain as a testimony for the generations to come, as I was instructed to do. Who am I?

ANSWERS:

1. C (2:1-10) 2. Moses (17:15-16) 3. A (2:15-19) 4. Aaron (32:22-24) 5. B (7:15) 6. C (8:18-19) 7. D (28:30) 8. Jethro, Moses' father-in-law (18:1,14) 9. from the people's gold earrings (32:2-3) 10. Amalekites (17:8) 11. Elim (15:27) 12. Aaron (16:32-34)

## SEEING THE SACRIFICES

**Burnt Offering (Lev. 6:8–13)** = Total death sacrifice of Christ—We are dead to self, alive in Christ.

**Grain Offering (Lev. 6:14–23)** = Firstfruits and tithes—We have provision and abundance in the Lord.

**Fellowship Offering (Lev. 7:11–21)** = Closeness and friendship with Jesus—We express thankfulness as children of God.

**Sin Offering (Lev. 6:24–30)** = Forgiveness for mistakes—God is faithful to forgive and cleanse us.

**Guilt Offering (Lev. 7:1–10)** = Restitution and repentance—We admit our guilt and receive restoration.

LIFE LESSONS: God gives firm instruction on how to come near to him (1:1–17).

### Ahhhhhh . . .

Every seven years the land was given a Sabbath rest—no crops were planted or grown so the land could rest (25:1-7).

### SEX MATTERS!

Biblical warnings about sexual impurity in the New Testament actually began in Leviticus. God cares. He created sex and set the boundaries (20:10-21).

LIFE LESSONS: God designed clear boundaries for sex (18:1–23). Take sin as seriously as God does (20:1–27).

# LEVITICUS

## DID YOU KNOW ?

▶ All the laws in Leviticus were given to Moses during the first year after the Exodus, as the people were camped at Mount Sinai.

▶ The Year of Jubilee occurred every 50 years. All debts were forgiven and lands were restored to their original family owners (25:8-55).

## The Wages of Sin?

Breaking the commandments in the Old Testament often brought death. God allowed this to show the truth about disobedience — **sin kills!**

### BY THE NUMBERS

**27** CHAPTERS

**858** VERSES

**22,013** WORDS

# LEVITICUS IN REVIEW

 **WHO DUNNIT?**

1. The son of an Egyptian father and an Israelite mother got into a fight; then he was stoned to death for blasphemy. What was his mother's name?

A. Shelomith

B. Deborah

C. Dibri

D. Hannah

 **THEN VS. NOW**

2. The Biblical term shekel was a measurement of weight. What would 20 shekels be in ounces today?

 **HOT SEAT**

3. Although I am not a human or animal, God said he would punish me for my sin. What am I?

A. The waters at Meribah

B. The sky

C. The ocean

D. The land

 **WHO DUNNIT?**

4. Abihu and his brother offered unauthorized fire in their censers, and they were destroyed. Who was their father?

 **MINUTIAE & MISCELLANY**

5. Who carried the bodies of Nadab and Abihu out of the camp?

A. Mishael and Elzaphan

B. Eleazar and Ithamar

C. Aaron and Moses

D. Joshua and Caleb

 **MINUTIAE & MISCELLANY**

6. When a woman became pregnant and gave birth, what was she required to bring to the priest for her offerings?

A. A year-old bull and a young lamb

B. Two doves and one young pigeon

C. A year-old lamb and a young pigeon or a dove

D. A year-old lamb and an ephah of grain

 **"?" CRYPTIC PHRASES**

7. Molek was a false god known for which characteristic?

A. Child sacrifice

B. Worship of gold

C. Nature worship

D. Majestic architecture

 **HOT SEAT**

8. The people of Israel cannot permanently sell their land because they are not the true owners of it. I am. Who am I?

A. The high priests

B. The Levites

C. Aaron's sons

D. God

 **MINUTIAE & MISCELLANY**

9. God said, "Observe my Sabbaths and have reverence for my_____."
(Fill in the blank.)

**WHERE IN THE WORLD**

10. Where were the Israelites camped during the giving of the laws that are included in the book of Leviticus?

**HOT SEAT**

11. In this book, I am the very last thing commanded to be brought in. What am I?

## What's the Cost?

Moses and Aaron both died in the desert before they reached the Promised Land because they disobeyed the Lord when Moses struck the rock for water (20:8–12). **Obedience pays!**

## 36 CHAPTERS

## 1,288 VERSES

## 28,141 WORDS

# NUMBERS

## THE LEADING of GOD

The cloud of the glory of God came on the tabernacle to lead it. When it settled, the Israelites camped; when it lifted, they broke camp and followed it. God guides his people!

## HUMBLE MOSES

Although Moses was the most humble man on the face of the earth (12:3), the Israelites accused him of bad leadership and rebelled against him at least ten times. They suffered the consequences of their actions. In most cases, Moses himself interceded for them, and God stopped the curse!

They complained about hardship; fire of the Lord burned among them (11:1-3).

They complained about food; they were struck with a severe plague (11:31-34).

Miriam and Aaron complained about Moses' wife; Miriam became leprous (12:1-15).

They grumbled about conditions; they received venomous snakes among them (21:4-9).

## DID YOU KNOW ?

▶ There were over 600,000 fighting men in Israel over the age of 20. Including women and children, there could have been well over three million people traveling together through the desert!

▶ Two complete censuses were taken, the first when the Israelites were given the law and the second after they had spent 40 years in the desert (1:2; 26:2).

▶ The events narrated in the book of Numbers describe what took place in the 38 years after the giving of the Law at Mount Sinai in Leviticus, up to Moses' speech in Deuteronomy.

# NUMBERS IN REVIEW

### 🔥 HOT SEAT
1. We are a clan of the Levite tribe responsible for carrying the curtains and covering of the tabernacle when we move about the desert. Who are we?

### Q WHO SAID IT?
2. "Rise up, Lord! May your enemies be scattered; may your foes flee before you."

### Q WHO SAID IT?
3. "We should go up and take possession of the land, for we can certainly do it."

### ⏱ TIME TRAVELER
4. You are a child of the rebellious generation that grumbled and said they could not take the promised land. You have been sent into the desert for 40 years while that grumbling generation dies off. What did God say you would be during that time?

A. A shepherd

B. Forsaken

C. A warrior

D. Destitute

### 🏹 WHO DUNNIT?
5. Who led a rebellion against Moses and Aaron but ended up "swallowed" by the earth?

### 🔥 HOT SEAT
6. I assisted Moses in leading the Israelites, then died and was buried at Kadesh, in the Desert of Zin. Who am I?

### Q WHO SAID IT?
7. "What have I done to you to make you beat me these three times?"

### "?" CRYPTIC PHRASES
8. Who was Baal of Peor?

A. Son of King Sihon

B. King of Moab

C. A false god

D. Balaam's servant

### Q WHO SAID IT?
9. "What have you done to me? I brought you to curse my enemies, but you have done nothing but bless them!"

### 🏆 MINUTIAE & MISCELLANY
10. At the end of their period of dedication, what are the Nazirites commanded to do after they bring their offerings before the Lord at the tent of meeting?

### 🏆 MINUTIAE & MISCELLANY
11. Aaron set up the lampstand in the temple according to the instructions God had given. Of what material was the lampstand made?

A. Gold

B. Silver

C. Bronze

D. Brass

### Q WHO SAID IT?
12. "God is not human, that he should lie, not a human being, that he should change his mind. Does he speak and then not act? Does he promise and not fulfill?"

## GOD RULES

It was not because of the righteousness of the Israelites that they took the Promised Land but because of the wickedness of the people there (9:4–6).

# DEUTERONOMY

## THE 40-YEAR JOURNEY

**The Incredible Deuteronomy Journey From Horeb to the Promised Land**
From Horeb to Kadesh Barnea to the hill country of the Amorites. Back toward the Red Sea, through Seir, past Moab, across the Zered Valley and through the Arnon Gorge. In all that time—for 40 years—God provided the Israelites with manna, water, clothes and sandals that did not wear out (29:5).

## DID YOU KNOW ?

▶ Moses' speech in Deuteronomy took place 39 years after the events in Leviticus and Numbers.

## THE AMAZING MOSES

"Moses was a hundred and twenty years old when he died, yet his eyes were not weak nor his strength gone" (34:7).

"Since then, no prophet has risen in Israel like Moses, whom the Lord knew face to face, who did all those signs and wonders the Lord sent him to do in Egypt—to Pharaoh and to all his officials and to his whole land. For no one has ever shown the mighty power or performed the awesome deeds that Moses did in the sight of all Israel" (34:10–12).

"Now Joshua son of Nun was filled with the spirit of wisdom because Moses had laid his hands on him. So the Israelites listened to him and did what the Lord had commanded Moses" (34:9).

## In the Word

The first ten chapters review previous events and commandments. Chapters 11–30 contain commands and reminders of how the Israelites were to serve God and enter the land ahead. Chapters 31–34 contain the selection of Joshua to lead the Israelites forward and the passing of Moses.

**BY THE NUMBERS**

34
CHAPTERS

959
VERSES

25,489
WORDS

# DEUTERONOMY IN REVIEW

 **MINUTIAE & MISCELLANY**

1. Which was not one of the cities of refuge Moses set aside, east of the Jordan, where anyone who had unintentionally killed a person could flee and be kept safe?
A. Bezer in the wilderness plateau
B. Beth Peor in the valley
C. Golan in Bashan
D. Ramoth in Gilead

 **MINUTIAE & MISCELLANY**

2. What did God instruct the tribes standing on Mount Ebal to do?
A. Pray for rain
B. Pronounce curses
C. Pray for fire
D. Defy the enemy armies

**THEN VS. NOW**

3. It took the Israelites 11 days to go from Horeb to Kadesh Barnea by the Mount Seir road. About how long would it take us to travel the same distance today by car?
A. Two hours
B. Two days
C. Seven hours
D. Seven days

 **HOT SEAT**

4. I've been known as everything from a criminal to royalty, but no one has ever had the mighty power or matched the awesome deeds I did. Who am I?

 **MINUTIAE & MISCELLANY**

5. If the Israelites lay siege to a city for a long time, fighting against it to capture it, what were they not supposed to destroy?
A. Fruit trees
B. Kings and princes
C. City walls
D. Daylight Savings Time

 **MINUTIAE & MISCELLANY**

6. How many years passed from the time the Israelites left Kadesh Barnea until they crossed the Zered Valley?
A. 20 years
B. 35 years
C. 38 years
D. 40 years

 **MINUTIAE & MISCELLANY**

7. God told the Israelites that he would bring terror and fear on all the nations under heaven because of them when Israel began to fight against whom?
A. The people of Seir
B. The king of the Moabites
C. The Ammonites
D. King Sihon of Heshbon

 **HOT SEAT**

8. Nun is my dad and Moses is my boss, but I will eventually take his position. Who am I?

 **TIME TRAVELER**

9. You are a future king of Israel. According to the instructions in Deuteronomy, what are you to carry with you on a scroll at all times?
A. The names of all the tribes of Israel
B. The law given to Moses
C. The song of Miriam
D. The list of your commanders and advisors

 **MINUTIAE & MISCELLANY**

10. When the people sinned by worshiping a golden calf and Moses broke the original tablets, how long did he then fast and pray for the people, that they would not be destroyed?

 **HOT SEAT**

11. I was cutting wood with my neighbor when the head flew off my ax and hit him, killing him. What an awful accident! The problem is, I'm afraid someone will kill me in a rage to avenge his death! Where can I go to be safe now?

**Q WHO SAID IT?**

12. "Has anyone built a new house and not yet begun to live in it? Let him go home, or he may die in battle and someone else may begin to live in it."
A. Moses
B. Aaron
C. Joshua
D. Army officers

# JOSHUA

## IN A NUTSHELL

Chapter 24 contains a recap of events from the time God called Abraham and blessed him *(24:1-15)*.

## What's in a Name?

The name Joshua is a variant of Jesus and means "salvation."

## A MAN OF HIS WORD

Even though the Gibeonites deceived Joshua when they met with him to establish a treaty, Joshua kept his vow before God and did not destroy them.

# FAMOUS
## JOSHUA QUOTE

*"But if serving the Lord seems undesirable to you, then choose for yourselves this day whom you will serve, whether the gods your ancestors served beyond the Euphrates, or the gods of the Amorites, in whose land you are living. But as for me and my household, we will serve the Lord" (24:15).*

### MIRACLES IN JOSHUA AS THE ISRAELITES DEFEATED THEIR ENEMIES

The Jordan parted, and the Israelites crossed on dry ground *(3:15–17)*.

Jericho's wall collapsed *(6:20)*.

The sun stood still for about a full day *(10:12–14)*.

# DID YOU KNOW ?

▶ **The book of Joshua chronicles the approximately 20 years of Joshua's leadership of the people after Moses anointed him at the end of Deuteronomy.**
*The Best Thing Since . . .*
Once the Israelites entered the land and began to eat of its fruit, the daily manna stopped. It had come to them all the years since they left Egypt until this day.

## A Significant Burial

The Israelites had promised Joseph they would take his bones to the Promised Land and bury them there *(Genesis 50:25; Exodus 13:19)*. "And Joseph's bones, which the Israelites had brought up from Egypt, were buried at Shechem in the tract of land that Jacob bought for a hundred pieces of silver from the sons of Hamor, the father of Shechem. This became the inheritance of Joseph's descendants" *(Joshua 24:32)*.

## BY THE NUMBERS

24 CHAPTERS

658 VERSES

16,232 WORDS

# JOSHUA IN REVIEW

 **MINUTIAE & MISCELLANY**

1. Whose bones "were buried at Shechem in the tract of land that [his father] bought for a hundred pieces of silver from the sons of Hamor, the father of Shechem"?

A. Abraham

B. Isaac

C. Joseph

D. Joshua

 **MINUTIAE & MISCELLANY**

2. Who was buried "in the land of his inheritance, at Timnath Serah in the hill country of Ephraim, north of Mount Gaash"?

A. Abraham

B. Isaac

C. Joseph

D. Joshua

**"?" CRYPTIC PHRASES**

3. The Kohathites, Gershonites and Merarites were subdivisions of which tribe?

A. Gad

B. Zebulun

C. Levi

D. Naphtali

 **WHO DUNNIT?**

4. Who placed the entire nation of Israel in danger of being defeated by its enemies by stealing a robe, gold and silver from the plunders of Jericho?

 **WHO SAID IT?**

5. "Come up and help me attack Gibeon, because it has made peace with Joshua and the Israelites."

A. Hoham, king of Hebron

B. Piram, king of Jarmuth

C. Adoni-Zedek, king of Jerusalem

D. Japhia, king of Lachish

 **WHERE IN THE WORLD**

6. When the Israelites broke camp to cross the Jordan and their feet touched the water's edge, the water stopped flowing and piled up at what town?

A. Jericho

B. Gibeon

C. Adam

D. Kiriath Jearim

 **WHO DUNNIT?**

7. These people approached the Israelites with dry, moldy bread, cracked wineskins and worn-out clothes, claiming they had come on a long journey. Once the Israelites had made a treaty with them, they discovered it was all a ruse, that they were actually close neighbors. Who are the deceivers?

 **WHO SAID IT?**

8. "Sun, stand still over Gibeon, and you, moon, over the Valley of Aijalon."

 **HOT SEAT**

9. We feel so special! Out of all the tribes of Israel, ours is the only one with land on both sides of the Jordan River! Who are we?

 **WHO SAID IT?**

10. "The land on which your feet have walked will be your inheritance and that of your children forever, because you have followed the Lord my God wholeheartedly."

 **TIME TRAVELER**

11. I helped assign territories to all the tribes of Israel. When I died, I was buried at Gibeah in the hill country of Ephraim. Who am I?

A. Aaron

B. Caleb

C. Eleazar

D. Elvis

 **MINUTIAE & MISCELLANY**

12. How many kings did the Israelites defeat on the west side of the Jordan?

# WITH GOD ALL THINGS ARE POSSIBLE

Gideon, a judge in Israel, defeated the entire Midian army with only 300 men—after sending the rest of his 32,000 soldiers home *(7:1-25)*.

# JUDGES

## When Will They Learn?

The Israelites would rebel against God and suffer oppression from an enemy. The people would then repent and call out to God, who would send a leader, or judge, to rescue them. Then they would have peace in the land . . . **until they rebelled again.**

## Nazirite

Samson was chosen by God and set apart to serve him before he was born. He tore apart an attacking lion with his bare hands *(14:5-6)*, captured and set fire to 300 foxes to burn up an enemy's field *(15:4-5)*, killed a thousand men with the jawbone of a donkey *(15:15)*, tore out the gates and doorposts of a city by hand *(16:3)*, and destroyed the temple of Dagon by pushing down the two main support pillars, collapsing the entire structure *(16:27-30)*.

## DID YOU KNOW ?

▶ Shamgar, a judge in Israel, killed 600 Philistines with an oxgoad, a sharp or metal-tipped stick used to drive oxen and cattle carrying heavy loads *(3:31)*.

▶ Sisera, an enemy of Israel, was killed by a woman who ran a tent peg through his head into the ground while he was sleeping *(4:21)*.

## BY THE NUMBERS

**21** CHAPTERS

**618** VERSES

**16,174** WORDS

# JUDGES IN REVIEW

 **TIME TRAVELER**
1. You just drove a tent peg through Sisera's head. What is your husband's name?

 **WHO SAID IT?**
2. "Draw your sword and kill me, so that they can't say, 'A woman killed him.' "

A. Heber

B. Abimelek

C. Eglon

D. Cushan-Rishathaim

 **TIME TRAVELER**
3. Your name is Othniel, and God raised you up as a deliverer for Israel. Who is your older brother?

 **MINUTIAE & MISCELLANY**
4. Who was the king of Canaan while Deborah was the judge of Israel?

**"?" CRYPTIC PHRASES**
5. When the people of Judah attacked the Canaanites, they advanced against the people living in Debir. What was Debir's former name?

A. Kiriath Arba

B. Ashkelon Jebus

C. Kiriath Sephir

D. Kenaz Hormah

 **MINUTIAE & MISCELLANY**
6. What word could the Ephraimites not pronounce correctly that cost them 42,000 men?

A. Shibboleth

B. Mephibosheth

C. Aroer

D. Peniel

 **HOT SEAT**
7. I am a Benjamite. After my tribe's rebellion, the rest of the Israelites had sworn that they would no longer give their daughters to be our wives. How did we acquire enough wives for ourselves after that happened?

A. Redeemed them with silver

B. Redeemed them with a young bull

C. Took them from neighboring nations

D. Caught women dancing and carried them off

 **TIME TRAVELER**
8. You, the king of Aram Naharaim, were just defeated by Othniel, judge of Israel, after keeping the Israelites as your subjects for eight years. Who are you?

 **WHERE IN THE WORLD**
9. In which city did a woman drop an upper millstone on Abimelek's head?

 **HOT SEAT**
10. I am the only judge of Israel noted as from the land of Zebulun. Who am I?

 **WHO DUNNIT?**
11. This man, the father of one of the judges, and his wife saw the angel of the Lord ascend toward heaven in the flame from a burnt offering. Who was he?

 **TIME TRAVELER**
12. You are a foreigner from the Valley of Sorek who betrayed Samson to his death. What was your reward for this achievement?

A. Silver

B. Gold

C. Position of authority in the land

D. Samson's properties

ANSWERS:
1. Heber (4:20-22) 2. B (9:50-55) 3. Caleb (1:13) 4. Jabin (4:23-24) 5. C (10:3-4) 6. A (12:6) 7. D (21:15-23) 8. Cushan-Rishathaim (3:8) 9. Thebez (9:50-53) 10. Elon (12:11-12) 11. Manoah (13:20-21) 12. A (16:4-5,18)

## What's in a Name?

Naomi requested that she be called Mara, which means "bitter," instead of Naomi, which means "pleasant," because of her suffering at the loss of her husband and sons. Her name remained Naomi, indicating God's continued blessing on her *(1:20–22)*.

# RUTH

## GOOD FROM BAD

God used a famine in Israel to send Elimelek, Naomi and their sons to Moab to eventually bring Ruth and Naomi back to Israel *(1:1–7)*.

## A GOOD MAN

Boaz not only showed favoritism by blessing Ruth; he was already known for his acts of kindness toward others *(2:20)*.

## GOOD CHOICES

Because she chose to go with Naomi and move to Israel instead of remaining in Moab, God blessed Ruth. She became the great-grandmother of King David and an ancestor of Joseph, the earthly father of Jesus.

## DID YOU KNOW?

▶ It is traditionally accepted that Boaz was the son of Rahab the prostitute, who saved the Israelite spies when they came to explore the Promised Land *(see Matthew 1:5, Joshua 2, 6:22-23)*.

### BY THE NUMBERS

4 CHAPTERS

85 VERSES

2,325 WORDS

# RUTH IN REVIEW

## ⏱ TIME TRAVELER
1. Due to a famine in the land, you left Bethlehem with your wife and two sons and went to live in Moab. What is your name?

## Q WHO SAID IT?
2. "I went away full, but the Lord has brought me back empty."

## ⭐ MINUTIAE & MISCELLANY
3. What event was happening when Naomi returned to Bethlehem?

A. Passover Festival

B. Festival of Tabernacles

C. Barley harvest

D. Full moon celebration

## 🏹 WHO DUNNIT?
4. Naomi sold the land that belonged to her husband Elimelek after she moved back to Bethlehem. Who bought it?

## ⭐ MINUTIAE & MISCELLANY
5. After finding Ruth at his feet, Boaz gave her something to take back to Naomi. What did he give her?

## 🔥 HOT SEAT
6. My grandson married a Moabite widow. Who am I?

## ⏱ TIME TRAVELER
7. Your wife decided to leave Naomi and stay in Moab. Who are you?

## ⬌ THEN VS. NOW
8. The night that Ruth met Boaz, she gleaned about an ephah of barley. Approximately how much is that in modern-day measurements?

A. 15 pounds

B. 10 pounds

C. 30 pounds

D. 16 tons

## Q WHO SAID IT?
9. "May the Lord deal with me, be it ever so severely, if even death separates you and me."

## "?" CRYPTIC PHRASES
10. When Naomi returned to Bethlehem, she told the people to call her Mara. What does this word mean?

## Q WHO SAID IT?
11. "On the day you buy the land from Naomi, you also acquire Ruth the Moabite, the dead man's widow, in order to maintain the name of the dead with his property."

## ⬌ THEN VS. NOW
12. In our current society, a financial transaction is considered completed with the signing of a contract or sometimes even a simple handshake. What constituted a finalized transaction in the time of Ruth?

ANSWERS:
1. Elimelek (1:1–2) 2. Naomi (1:21) 3. C (1:22) 4. Boaz (4:9) 5. barley (3:7–15) 6. Nahshon (4:20–21) 7. Kilion (1:2,5; 5:9–10) 8. C (2:17) 9. Ruth (1:16–17) 10. bitter (1:20) 11. Boaz (4:5) 12. One party took off his sandal and gave it to the other. (4:7)

## What's in a Name?

The name Samuel means "heard by God."

# 1 SAMUEL

## DID YOU KNOW ?

▶ The first king of Israel, Saul, eventually killed himself. David, his son-in-law and frequent enemy, then became king.

## Grass Is Greener?

*During Samuel's time as the last judge of Israel, the people began asking for a king. After trying to talk them out of it and explaining the burden an earthly king would impose, Samuel finally relented and anointed Saul, followed by David, as the first two kings of God's people.*

# TWO YOUTHS ONE GOD

Samuel was called by the voice of God in the temple as a child *(3:1–21)*, and he ruled Israel until the reign of King Saul began. David was anointed as future king as a young boy *(16:13)*, and later he killed Goliath with only his sling and a stone *(17:50)*. God blesses his children!

## A HIGHER CALLING

Samuel was dedicated to God by his mother before he was born. He was called by God as a young boy and served the Lord his entire life until he died at age 90. He was Israel's last judge.

## SERVICE AND SELECTION

Saul was rejected as king because of his disobedience to God *(13:14; 15:26)*. David was chosen as king because he loved God and obeyed him *(13:14; 16:7)*.

## THE LOST ARK

The Philistines captured the ark of the covenant in a battle with Israel, but they suffered so much calamity from having it that they eventually returned it—along with an offering to appease the God of Israel *(6:1–21)*.

## BY THE NUMBERS

**31** CHAPTERS

**810** VERSES

**22,273** WORDS

# 1 SAMUEL IN REVIEW

 **TIME TRAVELER**
1. Your granddaughter-in-law is barren. Who are you?

 **HOT SEAT**
2. At news of my death, my wife went into labor and bore a son but was overcome by the labor pains. Who am I?

 **WHO SAID IT?**
3. "I have sinned. Come back, David my son."

 **MINUTIAE & MISCELLANY**
4. Among David's wives was a woman named Abigail. What was her first husband's name?

 **HOT SEAT**
5. I was almost put to death because I ate honey! Who am I?

 **WHERE IN THE WORLD**
6. The first nation to attack Israel after Saul became king was Ammon. Which of the following tribes of Israel did Ammon border?

A. Judah

B. Asher

C. Naphtali

D. Gad

 **MINUTIAE & MISCELLANY**
7. In the battle during which Eli and his sons died, the Philistines took the ark of the covenant to their camp at Ashdod. How long was it before they returned the ark to the Israelites?

 **TIME TRAVELER**
8. You are the king of Gath and you are brought a man you recognize as David but who acts like he's insane in your presence. Who are you?

 **"?" CRYPTIC PHRASES**
9. Saul chased David around a mountain in the Desert of Maon that was later called Sela Hammahlekoth. What does that name mean?

 **MINUTIAE & MISCELLANY**
10. Two times David spared Saul's life when he could have killed him in his sleep. Which of the following was not among the items David took from Saul during those times?

A. The corner of his robe

B. His sword

C. His water jug

D. His spear

**WHO DUNNIT?**
11. What priest of Nob gave David and his men consecrated bread to eat?

**THEN VS. NOW**
12. How much did Goliath's armor weigh in modern-day measurements?

# 2 SAMUEL

## In the Word

In the lineage between Abraham and Christ, David is the halfway mark.

## THE TUMULTUOUS FAMILY OF DAVID

David himself, although a man of God, fell into sin and committed murder and adultery. His young son died as a result of his sin. Another of David's sons raped his own sister and was killed by his brother. Other sons attempted to overthrow David as king. Through it all, David kept his faith in God and emerged victorious.

## PROPHECY

God promised David that the Messiah, Christ, would come from his lineage: "Your house and your kingdom will endure forever before me; your throne will be established forever" (7:16).

## KINGLY KINDNESS

David showed great favor to a crippled man, Mephibosheth, who was the son of David's friend Jonathan. Mephibosheth always ate at David's table, along with the sons of the king, and was given all of Jonathan and Saul's land (9:1-13).

## DID YOU KNOW ?

▶ The books of 1 and 2 Samuel were originally combined and simply called the book of Samuel.

## BY THE NUMBERS

24 CHAPTERS

695 VERSES

18,793 WORDS

LIFE LESSONS: God has a better plan for your life than you might expect (2:4). Stop lust before it starts (11:1-5).

LIFE LESSONS: No challenge is too big for God to accomplish through you (8:1-14).

# 2 SAMUEL IN REVIEW

### Q WHO SAID IT?
1. "Today you have humiliated all your men, who have just saved your life and the lives of your sons and daughters and the lives of your wives and concubines. You love those who hate you and hate those who love you. You have made it clear today that the commanders and their men mean nothing to you."

### WHO DUNNIT?
2. Who was the steward of Saul's household who betrayed Saul's grandson Mephibosheth?

### TIME TRAVELER
3. You are a wealthy but aged man from Rogelim who provided for the king during his stay in Mahanaim. What is your name?

### WHO DUNNIT?
4. Who killed Amasa while greeting him with the phrase, "How are you, my brother?"

### WHO DUNNIT?
5. During the reign of David, there was a famine for three successive years. What caused the famine?

A. David had taken an unauthorized census.

B. Saul had tried to kill David.

C. Saul put the Gibeonites to death.

D. David had killed the Philistines.

### Q WHO SAID IT?
6. "Go up and build an altar to the Lord on the threshing floor of Araunah the Jebusite."

### WHO DUNNIT?
7. When Abner returned to serve David and help recognize him as king, who took him aside and murdered him?

### TIME TRAVELER
8. You are Obed-Edom the Gittite, and for three months the Lord blessed you and your entire household. By what means did he do that?

### Q WHO SAID IT?
9. Who said to King David, "Whatever you have in mind, go ahead and do it, for the Lord is with you"?

### TIME TRAVELER
10. You're the daughter of a king despising a king for dancing before the ark of the King. Who are you?

### WHERE IN THE WORLD
11. David became famous after he struck down eighteen thousand Edomites in the Valley of Salt. Where is that valley located?

A. The coast of the Mediterranean Sea

B. South of the Dead Sea

C. Along the Gulf of Aqaba

D. The shores of Lebanon

### Q WHO SAID IT?
12. "We have no share in David, no part in Jesse's son! Every man to his tent, Israel!"

## A PROPHET WITH A PURPOSE

God raised up the great prophet Elijah to turn Israel back to him and to oppose the evil king Ahab and his wife Jezebel *(21:20–25)*.

# 1 KINGS

## DID YOU KNOW ?

▶ The record of King David's life begins in 1 Samuel, continues through 2 Samuel and ends in 1 Kings. His son Solomon succeeded him as king *(2:10–12)*.

## THE KING WITH THE BLING

"King Solomon was greater in riches and wisdom than all the other kings of the earth" *(10:23)*.

## A Kingdom Divided (or North vs. South)

Solomon was the last king of a unified Israel. After his 40-year rule, his son Rehoboam succeeded him as king. But most of the people rebelled against his harsh leadership and followed Jeroboam instead as the king of Israel (the northern kingdom). Rehoboam reigned from Jerusalem as the king of Judah (the southern kingdom).

### On the Throne

During the time of 1 Kings, only two of the kings in power actually served God with all their hearts and did what was right in his sight: Asa, king of Judah *(15:11)*, and his son Jehoshaphat *(22:43)*. Ahab, king of Israel, held the distinction of committing more evil than any of the kings before him *(16:30)*.

### WHEN WILL THEY LEARN?

Repeating the idolatrous sin committed when they had left Egypt, God's people in the northern kingdom of Israel once again made golden calves to worship *(12:26–33)*.

## BY THE NUMBERS

22 CHAPTERS

816 VERSES

21,829 WORDS

## Walk the Walk

*Although God gave Solomon great wisdom, power and wealth, in later years he was led astray by his forbidden foreign wives and began to do evil in the eyes of the Lord. For that reason, most of the kingdom was taken from him, causing Israel to split into two nations with separate kings resulting in great conflict for many years (11:1–13).*

# 1 KINGS IN REVIEW

 **HOT SEAT**

1. The king of Israel was envious of my vineyard. His wife had me put to death when I wouldn't sell it to him. Who am I?

 **TIME TRAVELER**

2. During your reign over Israel, the people rebel against you and make another man king. Because of God's promise to your grandfather, you remain king over Judah, which has become a separate kingdom. Who are you?

 **WHO DUNNIT?**

3. Which son of David tried to make himself king but was overruled by David himself, who then made another of his sons king?

A. Absalom

B. Adonijah

C. Joab

D. Nathan

**THEN VS. NOW**

4. While Solomon was building the temple, he built ten movable stands of bronze. How wide were these stands in today's measurements?

A. 4 feet

B. 6 feet

C. 8 feet

D. 10 feet

 **HOT SEAT**

5. When I found out Solomon had been crowned king in David's place, I sent ambassadors to Solomon. Solomon asked me for cedars from the forests of Lebanon to help him build the temple. Who am I?

 **WHO DUNNIT?**

6. Who hid 100 of God's prophets in two caves so that Jezebel, queen of Israel, couldn't kill them?

A. Asa

B. Elijah

C. Obadiah

D. Jehoshaphat

 **TIME TRAVELER**

7. It was said of you, "I hate him because he never prophesies anything good about me, but always bad." Who are you?

 **MINUTIAE & MISCELLANY**

8. What person, who shared a name with a future king of Judah, was made the recorder during Solomon's reign?

 **TIME TRAVELER**

9. You were told by a prophet that God was going to split the kingdom of Israel into two kingdoms, and you fled to Egypt to avoid being killed by Israel's king. You later became king of Israel and reigned for 22 years. Who are you?

 **HOT SEAT**

10. When Joshua destroyed Jericho, God said that whoever rebuilt it would lose his oldest son for laying its foundation and his youngest son for setting up its gates. Unfortunately, this prophecy was fulfilled while I sat on the throne in Israel when Hiel rebuilt Jericho. Who am I?

 **HOT SEAT**

11. I told Ahab there would be a drought in the land, and then the Lord told me a place to go where ravens would feed me. Where is this place?

 **THEN VS. NOW**

12. While Solomon was king, he had a daily provision of 30 cors of flour. How much is that in pounds?

A. About 75 pounds

B. About 300 pounds

C. About 5,000 pounds

D. About 11,000 pounds

# 2 KINGS

## ON THE THRONE

The kings of the kingdom of Israel were from many different families, but the kings of the kingdom of Judah were all from the line of David.

## TIME CHANGE

During the reign of Hezekiah, God sent a miraculous sign of healing to the king by having the shadow move backward ten steps up the stairway of Ahaz (20:8-11).

## LOSING IT

*Because of their repeated rebellion and sin against the Lord, by the end of this book, both kingdoms had been taken into captivity by oppressors. First, the kingdom of Israel was taken over by Assyria (17:7-23); then the kingdom of Judah was taken over by Babylon (25:1-21).*

### SWING LOW

The prophet Elijah did not die but was taken up to heaven in a whirlwind with horses and a chariot of fire (2:11).

## DID YOU KNOW ?

▶ The books of 1 and 2 Kings were originally one book called The Book of the Kings.

## BY THE NUMBERS

25 CHAPTERS

719 VERSES

21,408 WORDS

## In the Word

Many of the books of the prophets in the Bible were written during the time of 2 Kings: Isaiah, Micah, Amos, Hosea, Zephaniah and Jeremiah specifically mention kings from this period.

# 2 KINGS IN REVIEW

## Q WHO SAID IT?

1. "Tell your master, 'This is what the Lord says: Do not be afraid of what you have heard—those words with which the underlings of the king of Assyria have blasphemed me. Listen! When he hears a certain report, I will make him want to return to his own country, and there I will have him cut down with the sword.' "

## ⏱ TIME TRAVELER

2. You were eight years old when you became king in Jerusalem, and you reigned 31 years. Who are you?

## ⭐ MINUTIAE & MISCELLANY

3. The morning after Elisha spoke, water flowed into the desert. From which direction did it flow?
A. From the direction of Moab
B. From the direction of Edom
C. From the direction of Dothan
D. From the direction of Egypt

## Q WHO SAID IT?

4. "Lord, the God of Israel, enthroned between the cherubim, you alone are God over all the kingdoms of the earth. You have made heaven and earth. Give ear, Lord, and hear; open your eyes, Lord, and see; listen to the words Sennacherib has sent to ridicule the living God."

## ⭐ MINUTIAE & MISCELLANY

5. When Josiah destroyed the high places that Solomon had built for Ashtoreth (the vile goddess of the Sidonians), Chemosh (the vile god of Moab) and Molek (the detestable god of the people of Ammon), he covered the sites with what?
A. Grass seed
B. Small stones and sand
C. Human bones
D. Astroturf

## Q WHO SAID IT?

6. "Go, wash yourself seven times in the Jordan, and your flesh will be restored and you will be cleansed."

## ⭐ MINUTIAE & MISCELLANY

7. What king of Judah did Awel-Marduk, king of Babylon, release from prison?

## ✗ WHO DUNNIT?

8. Who secretly accepted unauthorized gifts and therefore became leprous?

## 🔥 HOT SEAT

9. I am the king of a mighty nation at war with Israel. I tried to attack and defeat the Israelites, but that pesky Elisha kept warning them of our every move. My troops were struck with some kind of freak blindness, and Elisha led them straight to the king of Israel, who had the gall to feed them and send them home. I can't compete with that! Of what nation am I king?

## ⏱ TIME TRAVELER

10. You are the prophet Elisha in the nation of Israel. A neighboring king is ill and has sent to ask you if he will recover from the sickness. You answer that he will recover but will actually die. What do you mean by that?
A. You are instructed to deceive this evil king.
B. You are secretly planning an overthrow by Israel.
C. He will recover from the sickness but then be murdered.
D. You know this sickness will return later and kill him.

## ✗ WHO DUNNIT?

11. Who killed King Josiah at Megiddo?
A. Pharaoh Necho of Egypt
B. Pharaoh Ramses of Egypt
C. Jezebel, queen of Israel
D. Araunah the Jebusite

## ⏱ TIME TRAVELER

12. You are Jehoiachin, 18-year-old king of Judah. Why did your reign in Jerusalem end after only three months?
A. Surrender to Awel-Marduk, king of Babylon
B. Surrender to Nebuchadnezzar, king of Babylon
C. Killed by Awel-Marduk, king of Babylon
D. Killed by Nebuchadnezzar, king of Babylon

## DID YOU KNOW ?

▶ After the genealogy, 1 and 2 Chronicles cover the same time frame as 1 and 2 Samuel and 1 and 2 Kings.

**BY THE NUMBERS**

**29** CHAPTERS

**942** VERSES

**18,583** WORDS

# 1 CHRONICLES

## MERCY, MERCY

When David committed a sin and was given three options for his penalty, he chose to fall into God's hands instead of humans', trusting that God is more merciful than people *(21:11–13)*.

### In the Word

The books of 1 and 2 Chronicles were originally one book. It is traditionally believed that Ezra was the author.

### TEMPLE MINDED

Although David was forbidden to build the temple of God because he had shed blood as a warrior, he prepared his son Solomon to complete the task during his reign as king *(22:6-13)*.

**THROUGH THE AGES**

The records in this book include the genealogy of Judah that reaches beyond the time of the kings after the exile.

## DAVID'S WARRIORS

King David had mighty warriors who served in his army. Jashobeam killed 300 men with his spear in one encounter *(11:11)*, as did Abishai *(11:20)*. Benaiah killed a lion in a pit on a snowy day, as well as Moab's two mightiest warriors and an Egyptian who was seven-and-a-half feet tall *(11:22-25)*. One group was trained to shoot arrows or sling stones with both their right and their left hands *(12:1-2)*. Others also came and joined David, and they formed a mighty army for God *(12:22)*.

# 1 CHRONICLES IN REVIEW

 **HOT SEAT**

1. Not nice! When I died, my enemies took my head and armor and hung them in the temples of their gods. Who am I?

 **CRYPTIC PHRASES**

2. Who is the father of Zimran, Jokshan, Ishbak and Shuah?

 **WHO DUNNIT?**

3. What valiant warrior took only a club to battle a seven-and-a-half-foot Egyptian and then killed him with his own spear?

A. David

B. Solomon

C. Joab

D. Benaiah

 **MINUTIAE & MISCELLANY**

4. At one point, David decided to count how many fighting men he had. God didn't like this, so he gave David three options from which to choose for how he should be punished. Which of the following was not one of the three?

A. Three years of famine

B. Three months of being swept away by his enemies

C. Three weeks of earthquakes damaging the palace and surrounding houses

D. Three days of plague in the land

 **MINUTIAE & MISCELLANY**

5. When David was instructed by God to build an altar on the threshing floor of Araunah the Jebusite, how much gold did it take to purchase the field?

A. 15 pounds

B. 60 pounds

C. 300 pounds

D. 700 pounds

 **TIME TRAVELER**

6. You are the commander of David's royal army. Who are you?

 **WHERE IN THE WORLD**

7. Isaac's son Esau was the father of the nation of Edom. Which of the following describes the location of Edom?

A. Along the northern edge of Israel

B. Along the northern half of the east side of Israel

C. Along the southern half of the east side of Israel

D. Along the southern edge of Israel

 **WHO SAID IT?**

8. "May the Lord multiply his troops a hundred times over."

A. Joab

B. Nathan

C. David

D. Gad

 **MINUTIAE & MISCELLANY**

9. How many musicians did David have?

 **HOT SEAT**

10. David gave me his plans for the temple. Who am I?

 **THEN VS. NOW**

11. About 375 tons of gold was donated for the building of the temple. How much is that in the measurements of that time?

A. 10,000 talents and 10,000 darics

B. 100,000 talents and 1,000 darics

C. 5,000 talents and 10,000 darics

D. 50,000 talents and 10 darics

**WHO DUNNIT?**

12. Who struck down 300 men with a spear in one encounter and was made chief of the officers?

# 2 CHRONICLES

## IN FOCUS

This book primarily covers the kingdom of Judah from the time of King Solomon to the fall of Jerusalem to the Babylonians. It begins with the construction of the magnificent temple of God, and it ends with it set on fire and destroyed.

## In the Word

The books of 1 and 2 Chronicles were originally one book. It is traditionally believed that Ezra was the author.

## DID YOU KNOW ?

▶ Solomon ordered thousands of workers for the building of the temple in Jerusalem—150,000 stone cutters and carriers alone *(2:1-2)*. The temple was 90 feet long and 30 feet wide, and the entire interior was overlaid with gold *(3:3-4)*.

▶ Joash was the youngest king of Judah, beginning his reign at the age of seven. He reigned in Jerusalem for 40 years *(24:1)*.

## BY THE NUMBERS

**36** CHAPTERS

**822** VERSES

**23,623** WORDS

# KEY VERSE

*"If my people, who are called by my name, will humble themselves and pray and seek my face and turn from their wicked ways, then I will hear from heaven, and I will forgive their sin and will heal their land" (7:14).*

# 2 CHRONICLES IN REVIEW

 **WHO DUNNIT?**

1. Who was the king of Tyre who helped Solomon build the temple?

 **WHO SAID IT?**

2. When asked by the people to lighten the heavy load laid on them by his father, Rehoboam asked several men for advice. Who advised him by saying, "If you will be kind to these people and please them and give them a favorable answer, they will always be your servants"?

A. The young men who grew up with him

B. The elders

C. His chief advisors

D. The priests

**"?" CRYPTIC PHRASES**

3. Who or what is Mahalath?

 **WHO DUNNIT?**

4. Which king of Judah went with Ahab, king of Israel, to fight against Ramoth Gilead in the battle in which Ahab was killed?

 **TIME TRAVELER**

5. You are the king of Judah who was struck with a foot disease but still wouldn't turn to the Lord, and eventually you died from it. Who are you?

 **MINUTIAE & MISCELLANY**

6. While Rehoboam was king of Judah, Shishak, king of Egypt, came and carried off Solomon's gold shields for the temple guards. With what did Rehoboam replace the gold shields?

**HOT SEAT**

7. I was the king of Judah who restored the temple of God but turned against him when Jehoiada died. Who am I?

**Q WHO SAID IT?**

8. "I have found the Book of the Law in the temple of the Lord."

**"?" CRYPTIC PHRASES**

9. What was Eliakim?

A. A territory in Babylon

B. An Egyptian province

C. Original name of Jehoiakim

D. A priestly garment made of camel hair

 **MINUTIAE & MISCELLANY**

10. How many gold sprinkling bowls were made to be used in the temple?

A. 12 bowls

B. 70 bowls

C. 100 bowls

D. 1,000 bowls

 **MINUTIAE & MISCELLANY**

11. Of all the kings of Judah mentioned in 2 Chronicles, whose reign was the shortest, lasting only three months?

**TIME TRAVELER**

12. You are in Solomon's family tree, and your mother's name is Maakah. You became king of Judah and reigned for three years. You defeated the king of Israel, Jeroboam, even though the northern kingdom had twice as many troops as you did. God gave you the victory because you relied on him. Who are you?

ANSWERS:
1. Hiram (2:3–4) 2. B (10:6–8) 3. Rehoboam's wife (11:18) 4. Jehoshaphat (18:3–34) 5. Asa (16:12–13) 6. Bronze shields (12:9–10) 7. Joash (24:2,17–18) 8. Hilkiah the priest (34:15) 9. C (36:4) 10. C (4:8) 11. Jehoahaz (36:2–3) 12. Abijah (13:1–18)

# EZRA

## DID YOU **?** KNOW

▶ The rebuilding of the temple was delayed for several years by political opposition, but it was finally completed when the original order by King Cyrus was located.

▶ The Israelites' return to their homeland from captivity is often called the "second exodus."

## THE MAN EZRA

Was a direct descendant of Aaron *(7:1-5)*

Received the hand of the Lord on him *(7:6)*

Studied and obeyed God's Word *(7:10)*

Had the wisdom of God *(7:25)*

Prayed and wept bitterly *(10:1)*

Fasted and mourned for Israel *(10:6)*

Appointed men to positions of leadership *(10:16)*

## IN A NUTSHELL

About 70 years after the Babylonians captured Jerusalem and took the Israelites away into captivity, the kingdom of Persia defeated Babylon and allowed any Israelites to return to Jerusalem who chose to do so. They also returned 5,400 articles of gold and silver that the Babylonians had originally carried away from the temple in Jerusalem *(1:11)*.

## KEY EVENTS

Around 42,000 Israelites returned to their homes from captivity in Persia and gathered together in Jerusalem to rebuild the temple. Joshua and Zerubbabel led the first group; Ezra led the second group.

## BY THE NUMBERS

**10** CHAPTERS

**280** VERSES

**6,267** WORDS

# EZRA IN REVIEW

 **WHO DUNNIT?**
1. Who carried 5,400 silver and gold artifacts back to Jerusalem from Babylon?

 **HOT SEAT**
2. As King Cyrus's treasurer, I counted out all the gold and silver articles taken from Jerusalem. What is my name?

 **MINUTIAE & MISCELLANY**
3. Approximately how many men and women, including slaves, returned from Babylon?
A. 3,000
B. 70,000
C. 5,000
D. 50,000

 **TIME TRAVELER**
4. You are the only priest named who rebuilt the altar of the God of Israel. Who are you?

 **WHO DUNNIT?**
5. Which of the following kings of Persia was against the rebuilding of Jerusalem?
A. Cyrus
B. Darius
C. Artaxerxes
D. Xerxes

**"?"** **CRYPTIC PHRASES**
6. Who is Shealtiel?

 **MINUTIAE & MISCELLANY**
7. Who was king of Persia when the rebuilding of the temple was completed?

 **THEN VS. NOW**
8. The first thing the Israelites did after the temple was built was celebrate the Passover. At the time, it lasted seven days. Is it the same now?

 **HOT SEAT**
9. I am the father of Ezra, descended from Eleazar son of Aaron. What is my name?

 **MINUTIAE & MISCELLANY**
10. After Ezra returned to Jerusalem, the returned exiles made several burnt offerings to God. How many animals in all were sacrificed?

 **WHO SAID IT?**
11. "Our sins are higher than our heads and our guilt has reached to the heavens."
A. Ezra
B. Cyrus
C. Darius
D. Joshua

 **CRYPTIC PHRASES**
12. What are Shekaniah, Shelomith, Bigvai and Hakkatan?
A. Native bond servants to King Artaxerxes
B. Names of some of the people who returned with Ezra to Jerusalem
C. Specially designated areas within Jerusalem for returning exiles
D. Four rivers located primarily in Persia and Babylon

LIFE LESSONS: God answers big prayer requests (2:1–9). Focus on others' needs more than your own (5:1–19).

LIFE LESSONS: Do what is right in God's eyes, despite criticism and opposition (4:1–23).

## DID YOU KNOW?

▶ The rebuilding of the wall of Jerusalem in the face of such opposition was such a miracle that even Israel's enemies eventually recognized it was completed by the power of God (6:16).

# NEHEMIAH

## What's in a Name?

The name Nehemiah means "consoled" or "comforted."

## IN A NUTSHELL

The first seven chapters relate the rebuilding and completion of the wall of Jerusalem. The last six chapters contain the reading of the Law and the people's rededication to the Lord and to his Word.

## THE BOOK STOPS HERE

This is the last book of Old Testament history, ending just about 400 years before Christ's birth.

### BY THE NUMBERS

13 CHAPTERS

406 VERSES

9,506 WORDS

## Like Moses

Nehemiah was cupbearer to King Artaxerxes in Persia. Like Moses, he gave up the comforts of the kingly palace to serve the Lord. He left to rebuild Jerusalem, and he eventually served as governor of Jerusalem for 14 years.

## THE MAN NEHEMIAH

Wept and fasted for the struggles of his people (1:4)

Was deeply saddened by the ruined condition of Jerusalem (2:3)

Inspired the leaders in Jerusalem to rebuild its walls (2:17)

Rejected intruders who had no part in Jerusalem (2:20)

Organized defenses against the enemies of God during the building of the wall (4:13)

Encouraged the workers to resist the opposition and continue to build (4:14)

# NEHEMIAH IN REVIEW

 **WHO DUNNIT?**

1. Who did not oppose the rebuilding of Jerusalem?

A. Sanballat the Horonite

B. Tobiah the Ammonite

C. Eliashib the high priest

D. Geshem the Arab

 **WHO SAID IT?**

2. "What are those feeble Jews doing? Will they restore their wall? Will they offer sacrifices? Will they finish in a day? Can they bring the stones back to life from those heaps of rubble—burned as they are?"

 **TIME TRAVELER**

3. Nehemiah describes you as a man of integrity, that you fear God more than most people do. Who are you?

 **THEN VS. NOW**

4. The governor at the time gave the Israelite treasury 1,000 darics of gold. What would that weight be in our modern-day measurements?

 **WHO SAID IT?**

5. "What they are building—even a fox climbing up on it would break down their wall of stones!"

 **MINUTIAE & MISCELLANY**

6. How many singers were among those returning from captivity?

 **MINUTIAE & MISCELLANY**

7. Where did the people gather to hear Ezra read the Law of Moses?

A. At the entrance to the temple

B. In the square before the Water Gate

C. At the base of Mount Sinai

D. Along the top of the wall

 **WHO SAID IT?**

8. "Go and enjoy choice food and sweet drinks, and send some to those who have nothing prepared. This day is holy to our Lord. Do not grieve, for the joy of the Lord is your strength."

 **MINUTIAE & MISCELLANY**

9. When the people cast lots to see who was to live in Jerusalem and who could stay in their own towns, what percentage of people were chosen to live in Jerusalem?

A. 10 percent

B. 30 percent

C. 50 percent

D. 85 percent

 **MINUTIAE & MISCELLANY**

10. At the dedication of the wall of Jerusalem, two choirs were assigned to give thanks. Where were they instructed to sing before they took their places in the house of God?

A. At the entrance to the temple

B. In the square before the Water Gate

C. At the base of Mount Sinai

D. Along the top of the wall

 **WHO DUNNIT?**

11. In the house of God, there was a large room formerly used to store the grain offerings, incense, temple articles and also the tithes of grain, new wine and olive oil. When Nehemiah found out that someone was living in that room, he had the man's belongings thrown out and the room purified. Who was living in that room?

 **MINUTIAE & MISCELLANY**

12. In how many days was the wall completed?

A. 39 days

B. 52 days

C. 66 days

D. 180 days

## What's in a Name?

It is traditionally believed that the name Esther means "star" in Persian.

# ESTHER

## REMEMBERING

The Jewish holiday Purim began in the time of Esther as an annual celebration of God's deliverance of the Jews from their enemies (9:20–32).

## DID YOU KNOW?

▶ The pole Haman built (on which he was impaled) would stand about the same height as an eight- or nine-story building by today's standards (7:9–10).

▶ The story of Esther takes place in the middle of the time of the book of Ezra, after the first group of people returned from exile in Babylon, but before Ezra led the second group of people back to Jerusalem.

## In the Word

Although the book of Nehemiah records the return of many Jews to Judah, the story of Esther takes place among those who chose to remain exiled in Persia. It is the only Biblical record of that portion of the Israelites.

## BY THE NUMBERS

10 CHAPTERS

167 VERSES

5,147 WORDS

LIFE LESSONS: God orders everything to accomplish his purpose (4:14).

LIFE LESSONS: Use the power and influence God has given you to help people in need (4:16).

# ESTHER IN REVIEW

### "?" CRYPTIC PHRASES

1. What are Mehuman, Biztha, Harbona, Bigtha, Abagtha, Zethar and Karkas?

A. *Provinces under King Xerxes*

B. *Territories in Persia*

C. *Servants of King Xerxes*

D. *Beauty pageant runners-up*

### WHO DUNNIT?

2. Of the men Xerxes consulted when Vashti wouldn't come, which one spoke to the king?

A. *Memukan*

B. *Admatha*

C. *Karshena*

D. *Marsena*

### MINUTIAE & MISCELLANY

3. Who was the father of Haman?

### HOT SEAT

4. Although my nephew Mordecai later adopted her, I am Esther's biological father. Who am I?

### WHO DUNNIT?

5. What were the names of the two guys who conspired to assassinate King Xerxes?

### TIME TRAVELER

6. Oops! Your husband, Haman, is second in rank to the king. You and some of his friends suggested he set up the tall pole where he eventually died. What is your name?

### MINUTIAE & MISCELLANY

7. How many years passed between the time when Esther was made queen and when Haman decided to kill the Jews?

### THEN VS. NOW

8. In exchange for Xerxes making the decree that the Jews would be destroyed, Haman agreed to put 10,000 talents of silver in the royal treasury. How many pounds is that in today's measurements?

### Q WHO SAID IT?

9. Who led the king's horse carrying Mordecai, dressed in royal robes, through the city while saying, "This is what is done for the man the king delights to honor!"?

### WHO DUNNIT?

10. Who told Xerxes about the pole Haman had erected for Mordecai's impaling?

### MINUTIAE & MISCELLANY

11. King Xerxes ruled over how many provinces from India to Cush?

### "?" CRYPTIC PHRASES

12. What did it mean to "cast the pur"?

A. *Stoning the guilty in judgment*

B. *A selection system similar to dice*

C. *Shaping molten lead into weapons*

D. *Tossing happy kittens*

ANSWERS:
1. C (1:10) 2. A (1:16) 3. Hammedatha (3:1) 4. Abihail (2:15) 5. Bigthana and Teresh (2:21) 6. Zeresh (5:14; 7:10) 7. About eight years: Vashti was removed in Xerxes' third year (1:3); Esther received a year of beautification treatments before appearing before Xerxes, making it his fourth year when Esther was made queen (2:12); Haman plotted to kill all the Jews in Xerxes' twelfth year (3:7). 8. 750,000 pounds (3:9) 9. Haman (6:11) 10. Harbona (7:9) 11. 127 provinces (1:1) 12. B (9:24)

## BY THE NUMBERS

**42** CHAPTERS

**1,070** VERSES

**16,920** WORDS

# JOB

## What's in a Name?

The name for God used in the book of Job is Shaddai, which means "Almighty." The name Satan means "adversary." The name Job can mean "persecuted" or "repentant."

# INTEGRITY IN ACTION

Although Job lost everything—his wealth, his children, his health and even the support of his wife and friends—he never lost his faith in God but believed God would eventually redeem him.

# DID YOU KNOW ?

▶ This book is considered by most to be one of the oldest books of the Bible.

▶ Job assumed the role of priest for his family, offering sacrifices and praying for himself and his offspring (1:5).

# KEY VERSE

## "Though he slay me, yet will I hope in him"

(13:15).

# JOB IN REVIEW

 **MINUTIAE & MISCELLANY**
1. How many camels did Job own before he lost everything?

 **WHO SAID IT?**
2. "Your words are a blustering wind."

 **TIME TRAVELER**
3. Of Job's three friends, you are the one who is a Naamathite. Who are you?

 **MINUTIAE & MISCELLANY**
4. What does Job call his three friends?

A. Worthless physicians

B. Liars and deceivers

C. Backstabbers and traitors

D. Demented followers of Satan

 **HOT SEAT**
5. I was the first of Job's friends to speak. Who am I?

 **WHO SAID IT?**
6. "I must speak and find relief; I must open my lips and reply."

 **MINUTIAE & MISCELLANY**
7. When Job's friends initially saw him in his agony, they sat with him but didn't say anything. How long was it before someone broke the silence?

 **WHO DUNNIT?**
8. Who gave Job pieces of silver and gold rings after his trials ended?

A. God

B. Elihu

C. His wife

D. His brothers and sisters

 **WHO SAID IT?**
9. "Man is born to trouble."

**MINUTIAE & MISCELLANY**
10. How many bulls and rams were Job's three friends instructed by God to sacrifice for what they'd done?

**TIME TRAVELER**
11. You are the second daughter born to Job after his trials. Who are you?

**MINUTIAE & MISCELLANY**
12. How long does Job live after he is restored?

## In the Word

This book is actually five books in one. Book One is chapters 1–41; Book Two is chapters 42–72; Book Three is chapters 73–89; Book Four is chapters 90–106; Book Five is chapters 107–150.

# PSALMS

## AUTHOR! AUTHOR!

**There were numerous psalmists, including David, Solomon, Asaph, Moses, Ethan and the sons of Korah.**

# DID YOU ? KNOW

▶ Psalm 119 is a 22-stanza alphabetic acrostic poem. Each stanza includes eight verses, and each verse begins with the same letter of the Hebrew alphabet.

▶ Psalms contains both the longest chapter in the Bible (chapter 119, with 176 verses) and the shortest chapter (chapter 117, with only two verses).

## POPULAR MUSIC

Psalms is widely considered to be the most read book of the Old Testament.

### BY THE NUMBERS

150 CHAPTERS

2,461 VERSES

41,094 WORDS

# PSALMS IN REVIEW

 **MINUTIAE & MISCELLANY**

1. In Psalm 135, David praises God for the things he has done and specifically names three kings he struck down. Which of the following is not one of them?

A. Sihon, king of the Amorites

B. Pharaoh, king of Egypt

C. Og, king of Bashan

D. Eglon, king of Moab

**Q WHO SAID IT?**

2. "Unless the Lord builds the house, the builders labor in vain."

**WHO DUNNIT?**

3. Who wrote the psalm that says, "May the favor of the Lord our God rest on us"?

A. Asaph

B. The sons of Korah

C. Moses

D. David

**MINUTIAE & MISCELLANY**

4. David designed Psalm 59 to follow the tune of a different song. What is the name of that song?

A. The Death of the Son

B. Lilies

C. The Doe of the Morning

D. Do Not Destroy

**WHO DUNNIT?**

5. Who wrote the first 11 psalms of Book Three?

**MINUTIAE & MISCELLANY**

6. Are there any psalms with no noted author?

**Q WHO SAID IT?**

7. "Blessed are those who have learned to acclaim you, who walk in the light of your presence, Lord."

**⏱ TIME TRAVELER**

8. David is fleeing from you when he writes "Lord, how many are my foes!" Who are you?

**Q WHO SAID IT?**

9. "Restore us, O God; make your face shine on us, that we may be saved."

**WHO DUNNIT?**

10. Who wrote, "As the deer pants for streams of water, so my soul pants for you, my God"?

**🔥 HOT SEAT**

11. I wrote the psalm that contains the line "The Lord says to my Lord: 'Sit at my right hand until I make your enemies a footstool for your feet.' " Who am I?

**Q WHO SAID IT?**

12. "For he will deliver the needy who cry out, the afflicted who have no one to help."

# KEY VERSE

*"The fear of the LORD is the beginning of knowledge, but fools despise wisdom and instruction" (1:7).*

# PROVERBS

## DID YOU KNOW?

▶ This book had at least three authors, including Solomon, Agur and Lemuel.

## CREAM OF THE CROP

According to 1 Kings 4:32, Solomon wrote over 3,000 proverbs, but only around 800 are recorded in the book of Proverbs.

## COUNSELOR

Proverbs offers sound wisdom for all types of relationships, from dire warnings against adultery to the highest praise for men and women who wholeheartedly serve God.

## KEY WORDS

Key Words/Phrases and the Number of Times They Appear

**WISDOM** = 52 times

**KNOWLEDGE** = 38 times

**UNDERSTANDING** = 25 times

## BY THE NUMBERS

31 CHAPTERS

915 VERSES

14,208 WORDS

LIFE LESSONS: Don't let others take advantage of you or convince you to sin (1:10–19). Greed destroys (15:27).

LIFE LESSONS: God is the ultimate source of all wisdom (3:19). Living foolishly will result in tragedy and regret (9:13–18).

# PROVERBS IN REVIEW

 **MINUTIAE & MISCELLANY**

1. What kind of treasures have no lasting value?

 **WHO SAID IT?**

2. "Every word of God is flawless; he is a shield to those who take refuge in him."

 **WHO DUNNIT?**

3. King Lemuel wrote the first part of Proverbs 31. Who does it say taught him what he says there?

 **MINUTIAE & MISCELLANY**

4. In Proverbs 19:5, Solomon specifically names something that will not go unpunished. What is it?

**WHO SAID IT?**

5. "Through the blessing of the upright a city is exalted, but by the mouth of the wicked it is destroyed."

A. Lemuel

B. Solomon

C. Agur

D. David

 **MINUTIAE & MISCELLANY**

6. When Solomon said, "In the end it bites like a snake and poisons like a viper," what was he talking about?

A. The way of an adulteress

B. Wine

C. Folly

D. A sluggard's ways

 **THEN VS. NOW**

7. Proverbs 31:10–31 was originally written as an acrostic poem in the Hebrew language. Is it the same way in English translations?

 **MINUTIAE & MISCELLANY**

8. Agur wrote, "There are three things that are too amazing for me, four that I do not understand." Which of the following was not one of them?

A. The way of an eagle in the sky

B. The way of a ship on the high seas

C. The way of a man with a young woman

D. The way of a seed in the ground

 **WHO SAID IT?**

9. "Let's enjoy ourselves with love!"

 **MINUTIAE & MISCELLANY**

10. Who does Solomon describe as "swift to shed blood"?

A. Sinful men

B. The adulteress

C. Those who favor folly

D. One who devises wicked schemes

 **HOT SEAT**

11. I wrote "Speak up for those who cannot speak for themselves, for the rights of all who are destitute." Who am I?

 **MINUTIAE & MISCELLANY**

12. A godly woman considers a field and buys it; out of her earnings she plants what?

A. Garden

B. Crop

C. Vineyard

D. Orchard

## KEY WORDS

Key Words/Phrases and the
Number of Times They Appear

**Meaningless** = 35 times

**Under the sun:** = 29 times

**Wisdom:** = 26 times

# ECCLESIASTES

## MEET THE AUTHOR

King Solomon was King David's son and the third king of Israel. He had greater wisdom and more riches than anyone on earth. He also wrote 3,000 proverbs and 1,005 songs *(see 1 Kings 4:32)*.

## IN A NUTSHELL

King Solomon set out to test all that is done "under the sun" *(1:3)*, from riches to folly. He discovered that "everything was meaningless" *(2:11)* except to "fear God and keep his commandments, for this is the duty of all mankind" *(12:13)*.

## AGES OF WISDOM

It is traditionally believed that Solomon wrote Song of Songs in his youth, Proverbs in his middle years and Ecclesiastes in his old age.

## A Time and a Season

*Ecclesiastes 3:1–8 is one of the most quoted passages from this book.*

LIFE LESSONS: Don't waste your life on temporary thrills, excitement and fun (2:1–3).

LIFE LESSONS: A good friend is more valuable than money or possessions (4:9–12). Honoring God satisfies (12:13).

# ECCLESIASTES IN REVIEW

 **MINUTIAE & MISCELLANY**

1. "For with much wisdom comes much _____." Fill in the blank.

A. Knowledge

B. Sorrow

C. Respect

D. Joy

 **MINUTIAE & MISCELLANY**

2. Solomon says in Ecclesiastes 3:12 that there is nothing better for people than to what?

 **MINUTIAE & MISCELLANY**

3. In the place of justice what was there?

A. Wickedness

B. Mercy

C. Grace

D. Contempt

 **MINUTIAE & MISCELLANY**

4. According to Ecclesiastes 4:2, who was happier, the dead or the living?

**MINUTIAE & MISCELLANY**

5. What does the abundance of the rich permit them?

A. Exceeding happiness

B. Great understanding

C. Divine wisdom

D. No sleep

**MINUTIAE & MISCELLANY**

6. To what does Solomon compare the laughter of fools?

# SONG OF SONGS IN REVIEW

 **MINUTIAE & MISCELLANY**

1. To what does Solomon compare his beloved's eyes in Song of Songs 1:15?

 **THEN VS. NOW**

2. Solomon's beloved said that 200 shekels were for the tenders of her vineyard. What does that translate to in pounds?

 **MINUTIAE & MISCELLANY**

3. Solomon compares his beloved to a lily among thorns. What does she compare him to?

A. An apple tree among the trees of the forest

B. An eagle among sparrows

C. A cool stream in a desert

D. A mighty warrior among peasants

 **Q WHO SAID IT?**

4. "Come, south wind! Blow on my garden, that its fragrance may spread everywhere." Who said this—He, She or Friends?

 **WHERE IN THE WORLD**

5. To which mountain does Solomon compare his beloved's head in the Song of Songs?

A. Mount Hermon

B. Mount Carmel

C. Mount Sinai

D. Mount Nebo

 **Q WHO SAID IT?**

6. "Drink your fill of love." Who said this—He, She or Friends?

## WHAT DOES IT MEAN?

It is widely accepted that this is a love song that portrays not only a passionate romance between a man and a woman but also illustrates the never-ending passion Christ the King shows for his bride, the church.

# SONG OF SONGS

## LOVE AND SCIENCE

Solomon had an extensive knowledge of plants and animals, which is evident in this narrative that compares the charms and beauty of the woman to the magnificence of God's earthly creations.

### Love Story

Many aspects of real relationships are expressed, including attraction, devotion and admiration as well as separation, longing and desire.

## SAY, WHAT?

King Solomon was highly experienced at romance and relationships, having 700 wives and 300 concubines (*see 1 Kings 11:3*).

## THE PRESENTATION

This book is an arrangement featuring three main voices: the man, the woman and a chorus of friends. It is written in a style similar to a live presentation or a screenplay.

## BY THE NUMBERS

**8** CHAPTERS

**117** VERSES

**2,577** WORDS

# THE MAN ISAIAH

Isaiah was a prophet to the kingdom of Judah. He prophesied that Babylon would bring judgment on Judah almost 100 years before the Babylonian kingdom existed.

# ISAIAH

## What's in a Name?

The name Isaiah means "The LORD is salvation."

LIFE LESSONS: Pride will damage your relationship with God (2:11). Serve God with everything within you (6:8–13).

LIFE LESSONS: Trust Jesus as Savior of the world because he fulfilled ancient prophecies (53:12).

## IN A NUTSHELL

This book is often divided into two major sections. There are 66 chapters in Isaiah, the same as the number of books of the Bible. The message in the first 39 chapters relates to judgment and sin in humankind, and the 27 remaining chapters speak of redemption and forgiveness, themes found in both the Old and New testaments.

## MARTYRED BY MANASSEH?

It is traditionally believed that Isaiah died when he was sawn in half, possibly by King Manasseh.

## DID YOU KNOW?

▶ Isaiah is often referred to as "The Messianic Prophet" and his book called "The Gospel of Isaiah" because of his many references to the coming Messiah. The book of Isaiah contains more direct prophecies concerning Christ's coming than any other book of the Old Testament.

▶ The New Testament quotes Isaiah 75 times.

## BY THE NUMBERS

66 CHAPTERS

1,292 VERSES

34,401 WORDS

# ISAIAH IN REVIEW

 **"?" CRYPTIC PHRASES**

1. What are Kir and Ar?

A. Musical instruments

B. King Hezekiah's children

C. Headwater rivers in Assyria

D. Stronghold cities of Moab

 **HOT SEAT**

2. As king of Assyria, I started by invading Judah, then proceeded to Jerusalem. I mocked Hezekiah, and I mocked God—after all, I had the strength and military might to walk all over these people! But, as you probably guessed, I was defeated and died in my own country. Who am I?

**"?" CRYPTIC PHRASES**

3. "Bel bows down, Nebo stoops low," and they themselves go off to captivity. Who are they?

A. Kings of Tyre

B. Warriors from Assyria

C. Moabite eunuchs

D. Babylonian gods

 **TIME TRAVELER**

4. You are the palace administrator for Hezekiah, king of Judah. What is your name?

**"?" CRYPTIC PHRASES**

5. What is the meaning of the word Hephzibah?

A. In great distress

B. My delight is in her

C. The sinner who reaches

D. Would not be gathered

 **HOT SEAT**

6. I had a busy night! I am an angel of the Lord, and I was sent to destroy the Assyrian army advancing against Jerusalem. How many of them did I strike down before daybreak?

 **MINUTIAE & MISCELLANY**

7. What will be given the new name Hephzibah?

 **WHO DUNNIT?**

8. Who named their son Maher-Shalal-Hash-Baz?

A. King Uzziah

B. King Jotham

C. The prophet Isaiah

D. The prophet Uriah

 **MINUTIAE & MISCELLANY**

9. According to Isaiah's prophecies, who would "rule over" Jerusalem and Judah?

A. Assyrians

B. Babylonians

C. The wicked

D. Children

 **THEN VS. NOW**

10. Isaiah spoke of a cursed ten-acre vineyard that would only produce a bath of wine. How much is a bath in gallons?

**MINUTIAE & MISCELLANY**

11. Isaiah cursed Tyre and said it would be forgotten for several years, the span of a king's life. How long did he specify that would be?

A. 65 years

B. 70 years

C. 75 years

D. 80 years

 **WHO DUNNIT?**

12. These people were committing evil. They were practicing divination and idolatry. Isaiah asked God not to forgive them or raise them up. What is the name of this evil city or nation?

A. Tyre

B. Babylon

C. Israel

D. Assyria

## What's in a Name?

The name Jeremiah means "The Lord exalts." He has become known as "the weeping prophet" because of his deep sadness and heartbreak for the nation of Israel.

# JEREMIAH

## Can You Hear Me Now?

Jeremiah was called to serve God as a prophet before he was born *(1:5)*.

## A ROUGH ROAD AHEAD

Jeremiah prophesied that the people of Judah would be taken captive by Babylon and that they would be held for 70 years. The name Babylon (or Babylonia or Babylonian) is mentioned 207 times in the book of Jeremiah.

## A PERSEVERING PROPHET

Jeremiah was persecuted heavily throughout his life. He was threatened, put on trial, beaten, put in stocks, put in neck-irons, left to die in the mud at the bottom of a cistern and locked in a prison dungeon. Yet he didn't waver from his obedient service to God in proclaiming the word of the Lord to the people.

**BY THE NUMBERS**

52 CHAPTERS

1,364 VERSES

38,430 WORDS

# KEY VERSE

*"'For I know the plans I have for you,' declares the LORD, 'plans to prosper you and not to harm you, plans to give you hope and a future' " (29:11).*

# JEREMIAH IN REVIEW

 **WHO DUNNIT?**
1. Which king of Judah had Jeremiah thrown into a cistern?

 **TIME TRAVELER**
2. You are Jeremiah, and in your vision of a boiling pot tilted toward the nation of Israel, which direction are you looking?

 **THEN VS. NOW**
3. Jeremiah bought a field from his cousin for 17 shekels of silver. About how much is that in today's measurements?

A. 7 ounces

B. 10 ounces

C. 10 pounds

D. 30 pounds

 **HOT SEAT**
4. God says I am "deceitful above all things and beyond cure." What am I?

 **HOT SEAT**
5. I went around with Jeremiah, writing his prophecies on scrolls as he dictated them to me. Who am I?

 **MINUTIAE & MISCELLANY**
6. God instructed Jeremiah to buy something but then had him hide it in rocks. What was it?

 **WHO DUNNIT?**
7. When the Babylonians carried the people of Judah into exile, they left some of them in Judah with Gedaliah as governor until he was assassinated. Who assassinated him?

 **HOT SEAT**
8. That insolent Jeremiah sent a scroll he claimed was the Word of God warning us to repent, but as king of Judah, I defied the message and had the scroll burned, piece by piece. Who am I?

 **WHO DUNNIT?**
9. Who was the lying prophet who falsely claimed God would break the yoke of the king of Babylon and return the artifacts Nebuchadnezzar had stolen?

# LAMENTATIONS IN REVIEW

 **MINUTIAE & MISCELLANY**
1. Which of the following is not listed as a symptom of the suffering in Jerusalem?

A. Our dancing has turned to mourning.

B. The crown has fallen from our head.

C. Our feet have failed on our paths.

D. Joy is gone from our hearts.

 **TIME TRAVELER**
2. "After affliction and harsh labor," you have "gone into exile." Who are you?

 **WHO SAID IT?**
3. Who said about Jerusalem, "We have swallowed her up. This is the day we have waited for; we have lived to see it"?

A. Prophets

B. Priests

C. Enemies

D. Jericho

## THE WEEPING PROPHET

Jeremiah expressly wept and lamented the destruction of Jerusalem. This book is sometimes referred to as the "Funeral for Jerusalem."

# LAMENTATIONS

## DID YOU **?** KNOW

### IN A NUTSHELL

Jeremiah wrote this book during the beginning of the exile to Babylon, after the city of Jerusalem was destroyed.

▶ Each of the first four chapters is an acrostic poem, the verses of which begin with the successive letters of the Hebrew alphabet.

**BY THE NUMBERS**

5
CHAPTERS

154
VERSES

3,178
WORDS

## Heavenly Hope

In the midst of great destruction and condemnation, Jeremiah not only spoke of the nation's sin and punishment but also prayed for future mercy and restoration.

# KEY PASSAGE

*"Because of the LORD's great love we are not consumed, for his compassions never fail. They are new every morning; great is your faithfulness" (3:22-23).*

# EZEKIEL

## What's in a Name?

The name Ezekiel means "God will strengthen." Similarly, the message of the book of Ezekiel is one of repentance and restoration of the nation before God.

## BY THE NUMBERS

**48** CHAPTERS

**1,273** VERSES

**35,953** WORDS

## Heavenly Hope

Although Jerusalem had recently been destroyed and the people had been taken captive into Babylon, Ezekiel was given a vision of the future in which the temple and city of Jerusalem were rebuilt and the nation of Israel restored.

## DID YOU KNOW?

▶ Ezekiel was one of the Israelite exiles taken captive to Babylon, and he served as a prophet of God during the 70 years of captivity there.

▶ Ezekiel and Jeremiah's ministries overlap almost 30 years, while Daniel's ministry began before Ezekiel even appeared and continued later.

## MIRACLE LIFE

In the vision of the valley of dry bones (37:1–14), Ezekiel brought hope to the currently powerless people of Israel, telling them that they would once again experience newness of life and restoration through the power of God's Spirit.

# EZEKIEL IN REVIEW

 **WHERE IN THE WORLD**

1. Ezekiel's first vision was given to him while he lay by which river?

A. Pishon
B. Gihon
C. Tigris
D. Kebar

 **TIME TRAVELER**

2. When the Lord first called you, Ezekiel, he told you to eat a scroll. What did you say it tasted like?

 **THEN VS. NOW**

3. God told Ezekiel to lie on his left side for 390 days and to drink a sixth of a hin of water each of those days. How much is a hin?

A. 1 pint
B. 1 quart
C. 1 gallon
D. 1 cup

 **TIME TRAVELER**

4. God told you, Ezekiel, to shave your head and divide the hair into three portions. Which of the following was not one of the things God told you to do with the portions?

A. Scatter it to the wind
B. Burn it
C. Strike it with a sword all around the city
D. Drop it in the river

 **MINUTIAE & MISCELLANY**

5. "I will bring many nations against you, like the sea casting up its waves." Who is this about?

 **HOT SEAT**

6. God said that he would break both of my arms, one of which was already broken, and make my sword fall from me! Of what country am I king?

A. Egypt
B. Tyre
C. Assyria
D. Moab

 **TIME TRAVELER**

7. You, Ezekiel, are being carried around by God to show you the detestable things the people of Israel are doing. How is he carrying you?

A. By your arm
B. By your hair
C. By your feet
D. By your neck

 **MINUTIAE & MISCELLANY**

8. Who was God referring to when he said, "I will pour out my wrath on you and breathe out my fiery anger against you"?

A. Ammonites
B. Babylonians
C. Assyrians
D. Edomites

 **MINUTIAE & MISCELLANY**

9. Ezekiel compared Samaria and Jerusalem to two prostitutes named Oholah and Oholibah. Which one represents Jerusalem?

 **HOT SEAT**

10. Ezekiel told a parable about two eagles and a vine. I am the first eagle. What or who do I symbolize?

 **MINUTIAE & MISCELLANY**

11. The last verse of Ezekiel speaks of a city. What will that city be called one day?

A. Obadiah
B. The Lord is there
C. Presence of Angels
D. San Francisco

 **MINUTIAE & MISCELLANY**

12. What nation would God give to Nebuchadnezzar as his reward for defeating Tyre?

# What's in a Name?

The name Daniel means "The LORD is my judge."

# DANIEL

LIFE LESSONS: God rewards purity (1:8–21). Trust God and put your life in his hands (3:16–18).

LIFE LESSONS: Be prepared for whatever God asks of you, and use the gifts he's given you (5:1–29).

## Do You See What I See?

Daniel was anointed with messages from God, often in the form of dreams and visions. Nine of the chapters in Daniel refer to visions, dreams or other supernatural revelations from the Lord.

## A CAPTIVE AUDIENCE

Daniel was a prophet for the Lord. He was 16 years old when he was taken captive to Babylon, and he lived there throughout the entire 70-year time span of the Babylonian captivity.

## DID YOU KNOW ?

▶ It is traditionally believed that Daniel was over 80 years old when he was thrown into the lions' den.

## BY THE NUMBERS

12 CHAPTERS

357 VERSES

10,535 WORDS

## INTEGRITY IN ACTION

Daniel lived a pure life. The Bible doesn't record anything negative about him. "At this, the administrators and the satraps tried to find grounds for charges against Daniel in his conduct of government affairs, but they were unable to do so. They could find no corruption in him, because he was trustworthy and neither corrupt nor negligent *(6:4)*."

# DANIEL IN REVIEW

 **HOT SEAT**

1. I am one of four young friends taken captive from Judah and brought in to serve King Nebuchadnezzar. My old name was Hananiah. What new name have I been given?

**MINUTIAE & MISCELLANY**

2. Which of these was not one of the instruments played when everyone was to bow to Nebuchadnezzar's statue?

A. Cymbals

B. Flute

C. Harp

D. Horn

**WHO DUNNIT?**

3. Who told Daniel that King Nebuchadnezzar had a dream he wanted interpreted?

**MINUTIAE & MISCELLANY**

4. In the king's dream, he saw a statue made of several different things. What were the feet made of?

A. Gold and bronze

B. Silver and onyx

C. Iron and clay

D. Gold and silver

**THEN VS. NOW**

5. The statue Nebuchadnezzar had made was 60 cubits tall. If we measured it today with a yardstick, how many yards tall would it be?

**MINUTIAE & MISCELLANY**

6. Some of this book is in first-person narrative. Is it all from Daniel's point of view?

 **HOT SEAT**

7. I am the chief official who gave the four young men from Judah their new names. Who am I?

 **TIME TRAVELER**

8. You are Belshazzar. Are you any relation to Nebuchadnezzar?

**MINUTIAE & MISCELLANY**

9. When Darius became king, he appointed several satraps to rule throughout the kingdom. About how many were there?

A. 70 satraps

B. 90 satraps

C. 100 satraps

D. 120 satraps

 **TIME TRAVELER**

10. Sweet dreams! In your vision, Daniel, you see four beasts come out of the water. What does the third one look like?

A. A bear

B. A leopard

C. A lion

D. An eagle

**MINUTIAE & MISCELLANY**

11. When Daniel was told by Gabriel about the "seventy 'sevens,'" how long did he mourn?

A. Two weeks

B. Five days

C. A month

D. Three weeks

 **MINUTIAE & MISCELLANY**

12. What was written on the wall that needed to be interpreted?

A. Mar Mar Izith Dardal

B. Mene Mene Tekel Parsin

C. Moil Moil Embas Ovir

D. Do Wa Diddi Diddi Dum

## What's in a Name?

The name Hosea means "salvation." It is a derivative of the Hebrew word Hoshea, from which also come the names Joshua, Isaiah and Jesus.

# HOSEA

## DID YOU ? KNOW

▶ The life of Hosea is not mentioned anywhere in the Bible except in this book.

## LIVING LESSONS

In a dramatic illustration of Israel's unfaithfulness and ultimate rejection, God instructed Hosea to take an adulterous wife, representing the unfaithfulness of Israel to the Lord (1:2). After she was disgraced and renounced for her sinful ways, God instructed Hosea once again to receive her and forgive her, just as God would forgive and restore the nation of Israel (3:4-5). God named Hosea's three children to illustrate the condemnation and punishment of Israel for their sin: Jezreel means "God scatters," Lo-Ruhamah means "not loved" and Lo-Ammi means "not my people" (1:4-9).

# KEY VERSE

*"I will show my love to the one I called 'Not my loved one.'*
*I will say to those called 'Not my people,' 'You are my people';*
*and they will say, 'You are my God' " (2:23).*

## In the Word

The word sin appears 19 times in the book of Hosea. Prostitute (or prostitution) appears 12 times, and adultery (adulterous or adulterer) appears 9 times. The last chapter, however, still proclaims a message of repentance, forgiveness and restoration for those who would seek it.

## BY THE NUMBERS

14 CHAPTERS

197 VERSES

4,843 WORDS

# HOSEA IN REVIEW

 **HOT SEAT**
1. What a strange thing! My husband was instructed to marry me because I am a promiscuous woman. Who am I?

 **THEN VS. NOW**
2. Hosea bought his wife with "a homer and a lethek of barley." How much would that measurement be in today's pounds?

 **MINUTIAE & MISCELLANY**
3. "My people are destroyed from lack of _____."
(Fill in the blank.)

A. Sense

B. Knowledge

C. Righteousness

D. Gasoline

 **HOT SEAT**
4. When I was born, the Lord gave me a name that means "not my people." What is that name?

A. Jezreel

B. Lo-Ammi

C. Gomer

D. Hosea

 **MINUTIAE & MISCELLANY**
5. "When I found Israel, it was like finding _____ in the desert."
(Fill in the blank.)

 **TIME TRAVELER**
6. Your daughter-in-law is a prostitute, yet your son chose to marry her! What is your name?

 **MINUTIAE & MISCELLANY**
7. "I will be like the dew to Israel; he will blossom like a _____."
(Fill in the blank.)

 **HOT SEAT**
8. During the time that this word of the Lord came to me, there were four different kings in Judah. Which of these is not one of them?

A. Jehoash

B. Uzziah

C. Ahaz

D. Hezekiah

 **MINUTIAE & MISCELLANY**
9. "The ways of the Lord are right; the righteous walk in them, _____."
(Fill in the blank.)

A. And the godly will prevail

B. Although evil always fails

C. But the rebellious stumble in them

D. And soar on wings like eagles

 **"?" CRYPTIC PHRASES**
10. The name Bethel means "House of God." Beth Aven was used as a derogatory name for Bethel. What does it mean?

A. House of idolatry

B. House of wickedness

C. House of the avenger

D. House of the holy

 **HOT SEAT**
11. I am Hosea's daughter, Lo-Ruhamah. What does my name mean?

A. Makes music to the Lord

B. No longer despised

C. Not captive

D. Not loved

⭐ **MINUTIAE & MISCELLANY**
12. What will "spring up like poisonous weeds in a plowed field"?

A. Lawsuits

B. Strife

C. Enemies

D. Slinkies

## BY THE NUMBERS

**3**
CHAPTERS

**73**
VERSES

**1,839**
WORDS

# JOEL

## IN A NUTSHELL

Although the warning of Joel was of impending disaster, the message was of repentance and returning to the Lord (2:12–14).

## What's in a Name?

The name Joel means "the Lord is God." Joel was the son of Pethuel, whose name means "persuasion of God." The book is a prophecy of calamity, calling for the people to return to God.

## NOT KIDDING

It is believed that Joel prophesied during the time of King Joash, who was seven years old when he began to reign.

# KEY PASSAGE

"And afterward, I will pour out my Spirit on all people. Your sons and daughters will prophesy, your old men will dream dreams, your young men will see visions. Even on my servants, both men and women, I will pour out my Spirit in those days. I will show wonders in the heavens and on the earth, blood and fire and billows of smoke. The sun will be turned to darkness and the moon to blood before the coming of the great and dreadful day of the LORD. And everyone who calls on the name of the LORD will be saved." (2:28–32; see Acts 2:17–21, where this passage was quoted on the day of Pentecost).

# JOEL IN REVIEW

### "?" CRYPTIC PHRASES
1. What word is the name of a valley and means "the Lord judges"?

A. Jehoshaphat

B. Mediterranean

C. Sabean

D. Judy

### MINUTIAE & MISCELLANY
2. "Wake up, and weep you _____."
(Fill in the blank.)

### HOT SEAT
3. Some day we will be put on trial for scattering God's people and dividing up God's land. Who are we?

### HOT SEAT
4. God's people talked about us when they said, "A nation has invaded my land, a mighty army without number." Who are we?

### "?" CRYPTIC PHRASES
5. What did God say he would repay Israel for?

A. Lives lost

B. The years the locusts have eaten

C. What was destroyed in the earthquake

D. The grain offerings cut off from the house of the Lord

### MINUTIAE & MISCELLANY
6. According to Joel, which of these offerings has been cut off from the house of the Lord?

A. Grain offering

B. Fellowship offering

C. Burnt offering

D. Sin offering

### MINUTIAE & MISCELLANY
7. "I will sell your sons and daughters to the people of Judah, and they will sell them to the Sabeans." Which of the following was God not talking to when he said this?

A. Tyre

B. Sidon

C. Moab

D. Philistia

### HOT SEAT
8. The Lord has spoken to the nations to beat me into swords! What am I?

### MINUTIAE & MISCELLANY
9. "A nation has invaded my land, a mighty army without number; it has the teeth of a _____." (Fill in the blank.)

### HOT SEAT
10. After God pours out his Spirit on all people, he said we would dream dreams! Who are we?

A. Old men

B. Young men

C. Fighting men

D. Politicians

### MINUTIAE & MISCELLANY
11. According to Joel, who will be saved?

A. The priests and prophets of Israel

B. Descendants of the tribe of Judah

C. Everyone who calls on the name of the Lord

D. All who returned to Babylon and Assyria

### MINUTIAE & MISCELLANY
12. "In that day the mountains will drip new wine, and the hills will flow with milk; all the ravines of Judah will run with _____."
(Fill in the blank.)

A. Water

B. Blood

C. Cattle

D. Honey

# AMOS

### What's in a Name?

The name Amos means "to carry"
or "carried by God."

BY THE NUMBERS

**9**
CHAPTERS
**146**
VERSES
**3,796**
WORDS

## EQUIPPING THE CALLED

Amos did not have a background in ministry but was a shepherd
and farmer when God called him

to go prophesy to Israel

(7:14-15).

### A DARK DAY

It is believed that the event
documented in Amos 8:9 was a
prophetic prediction of a future
solar eclipse: " 'In that day,'
declares the Sovereign Lord, 'I
will make the sun go down at
noon and darken the earth
in broad daylight.' "

## DID YOU ? KNOW

▶ The last chapter
predicts both the fall of
Israel and its eventual restoration,
many years before the Assyrians took
the people of Israel captive.

# KEY VERSE

'The days are coming,' declares the Sovereign LORD, 'when I will
send a famine through the land—not a famine of food or a thirst
for water, but a famine of hearing the words of the LORD' " (8:11).

# AMOS IN REVIEW

### HOT SEAT
1. I told Amos to stop prophesying against Israel! After all, I am the priest and you'd think he would listen to me, but he keeps speaking against the king's sanctuary and the temple of the kingdom. Who am I?

### TIME TRAVELER
2. You are the king of Judah when Amos has this vision. What is your name?

### WHO SAID IT?
3. "I was neither a prophet nor the son of a prophet, but I was a shepherd, and I also took care of sycamore-fig trees."

A. Amaziah

B. Jeroboam

C. Amos

D. Cushites

### WHO DUNNIT?
4. What nation "pursued his brother with a sword," which caused God not to forgive even three or four of its sins?

### MINUTIAE & MISCELLANY
5. About which nation did God say, "The swift will not escape"?

A. Moab

B. Israel

C. Assyria

D. Babylonia

### MINUTIAE & MISCELLANY
6. Israel's "town that marches out a hundred strong" will have only how many people left?

A. 50 people

B. 10 people

C. 2 people

D. 25 people

### TIME TRAVELER
7. You are a mighty nation, but because you burned to ashes the bones of Edom's king, God has declared he will send a fire on you! Who are you?

### WHO SAID IT?
8. Who said to the king of Israel, "Amos is raising a conspiracy against you in the very heart of Israel. The land cannot bear all his words"?

A. Amaziah

B. Jeroboam

C. Israelites

D. Cushites

### MINUTIAE & MISCELLANY
9. "All the sinners among my people will die by _____." (Fill in the blank.)

### MINUTIAE & MISCELLANY
10. God told his people, "Many times I struck your gardens and vineyards, destroying them with blight and mildew." What did he say devoured their fig and olive trees?

### WHO SAID IT?
11. "Sovereign Lord, I beg you, stop! How can Jacob survive? He is so small!"

A. Amaziah

B. Jeroboam

C. Amos

D. Cushites

### "?" CRYPTIC PHRASES
12. The name "Lo Debar" means "nothing" in the following passage: "You who rejoice in the conquest of Lo Debar and say, 'Did we not take Karnaim by our own strength?'" What does "Karnaim" mean?

A. Horns

B. Weakness

C. Abundance

D. Chevrolet

## DID YOU KNOW ?

▶ This is the only book in the Old Testament with only one chapter. It is also the shortest book of the Old Testament with only 21 verses.

▶ Obadiah's entire prophecy is addressed to the nation of Edom.

# OBADIAH

## What's in a Name?

The name Obadiah means "servant of the LORD" or "worshiper of the LORD."

## DOWN AND OUT

### BY THE NUMBERS

1 CHAPTER

21 VERSES

575 WORDS

The nation of Edom descended from Esau, Jacob's brother. History records that Assyria and Babylon overran Edom, Israel and Judah during the same time period. But unlike God's chosen nation, Edom was never restored and completely disappeared from historical record at that time.

## THE SERVANT AND THE SIBLING

The descendants of Esau were condemned and the nation of Edom destroyed forever because of their continued violence against Jacob, or Israel (verse 10).

# OBADIAH IN REVIEW

### MINUTIAE & MISCELLANY
1. "The pride of your heart has _____ you." (Fill in the blank.)

### HOT SEAT
2. Obadiah says that I will be a fire on the day of the Lord. Who am I?
A. Judah
B. Jacob
C. Zion
D. Benjamin

### TIME TRAVELER
3. You are the nation descended from Esau. According to Obadiah, you will be turned to stubble. How many survivors will there be?

### MINUTIAE & MISCELLANY
4. "Those who eat your _____ will set a trap for you." (Fill in the blank.)

# JONAH IN REVIEW

### TIME TRAVELER
1. You are the residents of Nineveh. This crazy prophet came, preaching that you would be overthrown in just 40 days! How soon did you turn to God after Jonah started preaching?
A. 3 days
B. 7 days
C. The same day
D. 10 days

### HOT SEAT
2. Okay, so it was dumb to run from God, but I (Jonah) did it anyway. I wanted to get to Tarshish, so where did I go to find a ship that could take me there?

### MINUTIAE & MISCELLANY
3. How many days did it take to walk through Nineveh?

### TIME TRAVELER
4. "Tell us, who is responsible for making all this trouble for us? What kind of work do you do? Where do you come from? What is your country? From what people are you?"
A. People in Nineveh
B. People in Joppa
C. People in Tarshish
D. Sailors

### HOT SEAT
5. My son now tells this wild story about being thrown into the sea and somehow God sent a fish to swallow him up. Yeah, I know, crazy! Get this—he also claims he was inside the fish for three days before the fish just magically vomited him out on dry ground. I don't know what to think about this nonsense, but what can I do—I'm his father! What is my name?

### MINUTIAE & MISCELLANY
6. At least how many people lived in Nineveh?

### WHO SAID IT?
7. "I knew that you are a gracious and compassionate God, slow to anger and abounding in love, a God who relents from sending calamity."
A. King of Nineveh
B. Priest of Nineveh
C. Captain of the ship
D. Jonah

### HOT SEAT
8. When I (Jonah) was sinking into the heart of the ocean, I called out to God from "deep in the realm of the dead." What did I say was wrapped around my head?
A. My guilt
B. Praise
C. Both arms
D. Seaweed

ANSWERS:
OBADIAH: 1. deceived (verse 3) 2. B (verse 18) 3. There will be no survivors. (verse 18) 4. bread (verse 7)
JONAH: 1. C (3:4-5) 2. Joppa (1:3) 3. three days (3:3) 4. D (1:8) 5. Amittai (1:1) 6. 120,000 people (4:11)
7. D (4:2) 8. D (2:1,5)

## ON LOCATION

The story of Jonah is unique in that it takes place entirely in foreign lands rather than in Israel or Judah, unlike all the other books of the Prophets in the Bible.

# JONAH

## DID YOU ? KNOW

▶ The commonly told story of Jonah and the whale is actually a misconception. The passage in Jonah specifies that Jonah was swallowed by a huge fish—and technically a whale is not a fish but a mammal.

▶ Sailors today sometimes give the nickname "Jonah" to someone who brings bad luck.

### The Rest of the Story?
### (or Unmerciful Prophet)

After Jonah begrudgingly spoke the word of God to the Ninevites and they repented and turned to God, Jonah fumed in anger. We aren't told whether Jonah repented of his anger and lack of mercy. But we do know this: The salient message of Jonah is that God is merciful and compassionate and wants all people to repent and turn to him.

## In the Word

Even in his rebellion against God, Jonah's testimony to the sailors who threw him overboard caused them to call out to God and believe in him (1:16).

**JONAH TO JESUS** Jesus used the story of Jonah's three-day and three-night experience in the fish as an illustration of his death, burial and resurrection (see Matthew 12:40).

**BY THE NUMBERS**

**4** CHAPTERS

**48** VERSES

**1,200** WORDS

LIFE LESSONS: Don't try to escape God's calling on your life (1:1–9). God will protect you and guide you (1:17).

LIFE LESSONS: God's Word changes lives in unexpected ways (3:3–9).

# MICAH

## DID YOU KNOW ?

▶ This book covers a period of time spanning about 25 years under three different kings.

▶ Micah predicted both the exile to Babylon and the people of Judah's eventual return and restoration *(4:10).*

## BY THE NUMBERS

7 CHAPTERS

105 VERSES

2,825 WORDS

## NEAR AND FAR

Micah was a prophet under kings Jotham, Ahaz and Hezekiah of Judah *(1:1).* His message was concerning Judah and Samaria; however, it was addressed to all the peoples of the earth *(1:2).*

## What's In A Name?

Names and Their Meanings in *Micah 1:10–15*

MICAH means "who is like God?"

GATH sounds like Hebrew word for "tell."

BETH OPHRAH means "house of dust."

ZAANAN sounds like Hebrew word for "come out."

MAROTH sounds like Hebrew word for "bitter."

AKZIB means "deception."

MARESHAH sounds like Hebrew word for "conqueror."

# KEY VERSE

*"He has shown you, O mortal, what is good. And what does the LORD require of you? To act justly and to love mercy and to walk humbly with your God (6:8)."*

# MICAH IN REVIEW

 **HOT SEAT**

1. I (Micah) was given a vision from the Lord. Who was the vision specifically about?

A. Samaria and Jerusalem

B. Israel and Esau

C. Moab and Nineveh

D. Simon and Garfunkel

 **MINUTIAE & MISCELLANY**

2. Which prophecy about Jesus did Micah foretell?

A. He would have a virgin mother

B. He would be born in Bethlehem

C. He would ride into Jerusalem on a donkey

D. He would speak in parables

 **MINUTIAE & MISCELLANY**

3. What did the Lord say concerning the prophets who led his people astray?

A. They would not have visions.

B. They would be ashamed.

C. They would not have answers from God.

D. All the above

 **MINUTIAE & MISCELLANY**

4. What does God say he will do to Samaria?

A. Burn it to the ground

B. Turn it over to its enemies

C. Make it a heap of rubble

D. Cause large hailstones to fall on it

 **TIME TRAVELER**

5. You are standing where the sin of Daughter Zion began. Where are you?

**"?" CRYPTIC PHRASES**

6. What is Moresheth Gath?

A. A region in Moab

B. Valley located in Assyria

C. A town in Judah

D. A priest of Jerusalem

 **MINUTIAE & MISCELLANY**

7. What town will prove deceptive to the kings of Israel?

 **MINUTIAE & MISCELLANY**

8. Which of these is not mentioned by Micah as something for the people to remember from the past?

A. Moses, Aaron and Miriam leading them up out of Egypt

B. Joshua leading them against Jericho

C. What Balak, king of Moab, plotted

D. Their journey from Shittim to Gilgal

 **MINUTIAE & MISCELLANY**

9. In the last days, where will the law go out from?

 **MINUTIAE & MISCELLANY**

10. To where will the nobles of Israel flee when the conqueror comes against them?

 **MINUTIAE & MISCELLANY**

11. According to Micah, I can no longer be trusted! Who am I?

## IN LIKE A FLOOD

*Historians record that the walls of Nineveh were damaged during an overflow of the Tigris River, allowing the Babylonians to invade and conquer. This fulfills the word of prophecy in Nahum 1:8: "But with an overwhelming flood he will make an end of Nineveh."*

# NAHUM

## What's in a Name?

The name Nahum means "comforter."

# DID YOU ? KNOW

▶ Although Nineveh repented at the preaching of Jonah, it was eventually destroyed as predicted in the book of Nahum, at least 100 years after Jonah's visit.

## In the Word

Nahum's prophecy is addressed to the city of Nineveh, the capital city of Assyria. The book of Nahum predicts the fall of Nineveh and the entire kingdom of Assyria. The Assyrians had overrun and taken captive the nation of Israel.

## THE MIGHTY FALL

Historians believe that Nineveh had become the mightiest city on earth, with walls 100 feet high, a 60-foot moat, aqueducts, irrigation canals and enough stored rations to withstand a 20-year siege. The ruins of Nineveh still exist in the modern-day country of Iraq.

## BY THE NUMBERS

**3** CHAPTERS

**47** VERSES

**1,112** WORDS

## NAHUM IN REVIEW

 **HOT SEAT**
1. I am the great city Nineveh, yet that prophet Nahum calls me the city of what?

 **MINUTIAE & MISCELLANY**
2. "The Lord is slow to anger but _____." (Fill in the blank.)

A. Swift to avenge

B. Great in power

C. Quick to forgive

D. Faithful in righteousness

 **WHERE IN THE WORLD**
3. Nahum compares Nineveh to a city called Thebes. Where is Thebes located?

 **MINUTIAE & MISCELLANY**
4. "His wrath is poured out like _____."
(Fill in the blank.)

A. Blood

B. Wine

C. Fire

D. Water

 **HOT SEAT**
5. I am the great city Nineveh! Yet what does that prophet Nahum say my guards and officials are like?

 **TIME TRAVELER**
6. You are a soldier as described in Nahum. What color are your shields?

## HABAKKUK IN REVIEW

 **TIME TRAVELER**
1. You are a ruthless and impetuous nation of people, who sweep across the whole earth to seize dwellings not their own. Who are you?

 **HOT SEAT**
2. I am a horseman in the Babylonian army. How fast are my horses?

A. Swifter than leopards

B. Faster than the dawn

C. Quicker than lightning

D. Speedier than the rains

 **MINUTIAE & MISCELLANY**
3. What does Habakkuk say the earth will be filled with?

A. The blood of the warriors of light

B. The knowledge of the glory of the Lord

C. An army of locusts from the eastern winds

D. The cattle on a thousand hills

 **MINUTIAE & MISCELLANY**
4. "Woe to him who builds a city with _____."
(Fill in the blank.)

 **TIME TRAVELER**
5. You are a man who has built his "house by unjust gain." You have "plotted the ruin of many peoples, shaming your own house." What will the stones of your walls do?

A. Crumble to dust

B. Fall upon you

C. Seek abundant gain

D. Cry out

 **MINUTIAE & MISCELLANY**
6. "The Sovereign Lord is my strength; he makes my feet like the feet of a _____."
(Fill in the blank.)

## BY THE NUMBERS

**3** CHAPTERS

**56** VERSES

**1,319** WORDS

## What's in a Name?

The name Habakkuk means to "embrace" or "wrestle." In his book, Habakkuk wrestled with the sins and injustices in the world at that time *(1:1–4)*.

# HABAKKUK

## In the Word

Habakkuk cried out to God against his people's violence, injustice and disregard for the Law. In response God told him of the eventual invasion by the Babylonians and the resulting captivity of the people of Judah *(1:1–11)*.

## SONG OF THE SEER

Chapter 3 of Habakkuk's prophecy was quite possibly written as a song. "For the director of music. On my stringed instruments" *(3:19)*.

## DID YOU KNOW ?

▶ Daniel, Shadrach, Meshach and Abednego would have been among the first people of Judah taken captive in the siege by Babylon predicted by Habakkuk.

# KEY PASSAGE

*"Though the fig tree does not bud and there are no grapes on the vines, though the olive crop fails and the fields produce no food, though there are no sheep in the pen and no cattle in the stalls, yet I will rejoice in the LORD, I will be joyful in God my Savior. The Sovereign LORD is my strength; he makes my feet like the feet of a deer, he enables me to tread on the heights" (3:17–19).*

## What's in a Name?

The name Zephaniah means "The LORD has hidden."

## ROYALTY IN THE HOUSE

Zephaniah was a direct descendant of King Hezekiah, who was a godly king and prayed to the Lord. Zephaniah is the only prophet noted in the Bible as a descendant of a royal family.

# ZEPHANIAH

# KEY PASSAGE

*"The LORD has taken away your punishment, he has turned back your enemy. The LORD, the King of Israel, is with you; never again will you fear any harm. On that day they will say to Jerusalem, 'Do not fear, Zion; do not let your hands hang limp. The LORD your God is with you, the Mighty Warrior who saves. He will take great delight in you; in his love he will no longer rebuke you, but will rejoice over you with singing' " (3:15–17).*

## BY THE NUMBERS

3
CHAPTERS

53
VERSES

1,510
WORDS

## DID YOU KNOW?

▶ Zephaniah was a prophet during the reign of Josiah, who was eight years old when he became king in Jerusalem *(1:1; see 2 Kings 22:1).*

## In the Word

Zephaniah's prophecy begins with destruction over the whole earth as judgment for sin *(1:2–3)* but ends with restoration and healing for the nation of Israel *(3:9–20).*

# ZEPHANIAH IN REVIEW

 **HOT SEAT**

1. I am being called a "shameful nation" by that prophet Zephaniah! What nation am I?

 **TIME TRAVELER**

2. You are King Hezekiah's grandson. What relation are you to Zephaniah?

A. His father

B. His grandfather

C. His great-grandfather

D. His great-great-grandfather

 **MINUTIAE & MISCELLANY**

3. What land will belong to the remnant of Judah?

A. Moab

B. Ammon

C. Cush

D. Philistia

Q **WHO SAID IT?**

4. "I am the one! And there is none besides me."

 **MINUTIAE & MISCELLANY**

5. Concerning Moab and Ammon, God declared that one would become like Sodom, the other like Gomorrah. Which one was to become like Gomorrah?

 **WHERE IN THE WORLD**

6. "Gaza will be abandoned and Ashkelon left in ruins." To what nation did these cities belong?

# HAGGAI IN REVIEW

 **MINUTIAE & MISCELLANY**

1. Who was king of Persia when Haggai received word from the Lord?

 **HOT SEAT**

2. The word of the Lord came through the prophet Haggai to the high priest and to me, governor of Judah. What is my name?

 **TIME TRAVELER**

3. You are the high priest when the time comes to rebuild the Lord's house. Who are you?

 **HOT SEAT**

4. Well, as you can imagine, I'm a pretty proud father! I am watching my son as he receives the word of the Lord and carries out his duties as governor of Judah. What is my name?

 **MINUTIAE & MISCELLANY**

5. In what year of the king of Persia's reign did all this take place?

A. His first year

B. His second year

C. His third year

D. His fourth year

 **MINUTIAE & MISCELLANY**

6. Whom did God choose to be like his "signet ring"?

# HAGGAI

HAGGAI

## What's in a Name?

The name Haggai means "festival" or "feast."

**BY THE NUMBERS**

**2** CHAPTERS

**38** VERSES

**1,025** WORDS

### In the Word

Haggai, along with Zechariah, returned to Jerusalem and encouraged the returned remnant to complete the rebuilding of the temple.

## DID YOU KNOW?

▶ The rebuilding of the temple took 20 years to complete, mostly due to political opposition. There were actually only six years of work involved in the rebuilding—the other 14 years consisted of delays.

▶ Haggai is the second shortest book in the Old Testament. Only Obadiah is shorter.

## KEY PASSAGE

*"This is what the LORD Almighty says: 'In a little while I will once more shake the heavens and the earth, the sea and the dry land. I will shake all nations, and what is desired by all nations will come, and I will fill this house with glory,' says the LORD Almighty. 'The silver is mine and the gold is mine,' declares the LORD Almighty. 'The glory of this present house will be greater than the glory of the former house,' says the LORD Almighty. 'And in this place I will grant peace,' declares the LORD Almighty (2:6–9)."*

# KEY VERSE

*"On that day a fountain will be opened to the house of David and the inhabitants of Jerusalem, to cleanse them from sin and impurity" (13:1).*

# ZECHARIAH

## What's in a Name?

The name Zechariah means "the LORD remembers."

## INSPIRATIONS

### Zechariah related nine different supernatural visions given to him regarding the rebuilding of the nation of Israel.

## In the Word

▶ Several prophetic references to the Messiah are found in Zechariah: Jesus' triumphal entry, riding on a donkey *(9:9)*; Jesus, pierced on the cross *(12:10)*; the arrest of Jesus and the scattering of his disciples *(13:7)*.

▶ Zechariah and Haggai were both written to encourage the returned remnant of Israel to complete the rebuilding of the temple and serve the Lord.

## BY THE NUMBERS

14 CHAPTERS

211 VERSES

5,590 WORDS

# ZECHARIAH IN REVIEW

 **TIME TRAVELER**
1. You are Zechariah the prophet. God gave you the word, "Not by might nor by power, but by my Spirit." Who are you to give this message to?

 **MINUTIAE & MISCELLANY**
2. Zechariah saw a man standing among myrtle trees, and behind him were horses of three different colors. Which of the following was not one of the colors?
A. Red
B. Black
C. Brown
D. White

 **HOT SEAT**
3. My son is Berekiah, and his son is Zechariah the prophet. What is my name?

 **HOT SEAT**
4. I (Zechariah) saw a solid gold lampstand with a tree on each side. What kind of trees do I see?

 **TIME TRAVELER**
5. In Zechariah, what does God say Jerusalem will be called?

 **TIME TRAVELER**
6. You (Zechariah) looked up again, and there before you were "four chariots coming out from between two mountains." What were the mountains made of?

 **MINUTIAE & MISCELLANY**
7. What does God say will make the young men thrive?

 **TIME TRAVELER**
8. You are the staff that represents the family bond of Israel and Judah. What is your name?

 **MINUTIAE & MISCELLANY**
9. How much of the population of the land does God say will be struck down and perish?
A. One-fourth of the people
B. Three-fifths of the people
C. Two-thirds of the people
D. One-half of the people

# MALACHI IN REVIEW

 **TIME TRAVELER**
1. God said he would leave Edom's inheritance to you. Who are you?
A. Prophets of Israel
B. The desert jackals
C. Children of Israel
D. Sons of Pharaoh

 **HOT SEAT**
2. I am what the one true God seeks. What am I?
A. Godly offspring
B. Righteousness
C. Forgiveness
D. Sacrifice

**MINUTIAE & MISCELLANY**
3. God says he will be quick to testify against three things. Which of the following is not one of them?
A. Sorcerers
B. Adulterers
C. Oppressors of the fatherless
D. Those who are stumbling blocks

## What's in a Name?

The name Malachi means "messenger."

## ACROSS THE GAP

The book of Malachi is a prelude to the 400 years of prophetic silence broken finally by the words of the next prophet, John the Baptist (3:1).

4 CHAPTERS

55 VERSES

1,671 WORDS

# MALACHI

## JACOB OVER ESAU

The word given to Malachi confirmed the message that the nation of Edom, the descendants of Esau, was destroyed and would not be rebuilt.

## TO THE PEOPLE

The message given to Malachi was to turn the hearts of the people back to God and away from their sins. Specifically condemned were contempt, partiality, idolatry, adultery, divorce, sorcery, greed and stealing.

## In the Word

▶ Several passages in this last book of the Old Testament predict the coming of one who would arrive in the spirit and power of Elijah to restore Israel. In the New Testament, these references are mentioned with the coming of John the Baptist, who prepared the way for the Messiah, Jesus.

▶ "'I will send my messenger, who will prepare the way before me. Then suddenly the Lord you are seeking will come to his temple; the messenger of the covenant, whom you desire, will come,' says the LORD Almighty" (3:1).

▶ "See, I will send the prophet Elijah to you before that great and dreadful day of the LORD comes. He will turn the hearts of the parents to their children, and the hearts of the children to their parents; or else I will come and strike the land with total destruction" (4:5–6).

# THE NEW TESTAMENT

## What's In A Name?

MATTHEW = "gift of God"

JESUS (Greek form of Joshua) = "the Lord saves"

MESSIAH (Hebrew) = "Anointed One"

CHRIST (Greek) = "Anointed One"

# MATTHEW

## DID YOU KNOW ?

▶ When Jesus called Matthew to leave his position and become a disciple, he was a tax collector, considered one of the most sinful and corrupt vocations of the time.

## BY THE NUMBERS

28 CHAPTERS

1,071 VERSES

22,596 WORDS

## CONNECTING THE DOTS

As the first book of the New Testament, Matthew establishes Jesus as the Messiah from the point of view of the Jews. Jesus was a descendant of David—the earthly lineage prophesied in the Old Testament. The book of Matthew often references the Old Testament, which foretells the Messiah's arrival. The phrase Son of David appears 10 times; Son of Man appears 30 times; kingdom of heaven appears 32 times; and the word prophet (or prophecy) appears 41 times.

## In the Word

▶ This Gospel was written by a Jew to all the Jews, announcing the arrival of the Messiah as prophesied in the Old Testament.

▶ This Gospel contains over 60 prophetic quotes from the Old Testament.

# MATTHEW IN REVIEW

 **TIME TRAVELER**

1. Your grandson was husband of Mary, the mother of the Messiah. Who are you?

 **MINUTIAE & MISCELLANY**

2. How many generations were there from Abraham to Jesus?

A. 96 generations

B. 70 generations

C. 77 generations

D. 42 generations

 **HOT SEAT**

3. Hey, I am a peacemaker! What does Jesus say about peacemakers?

A. They will inherit the earth.

B. They will see God.

C. They will be called children of God.

D. Theirs is the kingdom of heaven.

 **TIME TRAVELER**

4. Jesus warned about you, a false prophet! He describes you as one who comes in sheep's clothing, but inside you are what?

A. A ferocious wolf

B. A hungry lion

C. A cunning serpent

D. A destructive demon

 **TIME TRAVELER**

5. You are just a simple human, but Jesus says you are worth more than many what?

 **HOT SEAT**

6. I am trying to grow a crop, but someone has planted weeds in my fields. I can't believe it! Do you know what crop I was trying to grow before the enemy stepped in?

 **HOT SEAT**

7. I am Herod's brother, and my wife is named Herodias. Who am I?

 **WHO SAID IT?**

8. "Lord, how many times shall I forgive my brother or sister who sins against me?"

 **HOT SEAT**

9. Jesus healed a blind and mute demon-possessed man, and the Pharisees said Jesus healed him by my power, not God's power! I am the prince of demons. What is my name?

 **THEN VS. NOW**

10. While Jesus was on the cross, he cried out "Eli, Eli." What does Eli (sometimes translated as Eloi) translate to in modern-day English?

 **TIME TRAVELER**

11. Your sons were fishermen whom Jesus called to follow him. One of them was given a name meaning "rock." What is your name?

 **HOT SEAT**

12. During the transfiguration, I offered to set up shelters for Jesus, Moses and Elijah. Who am I?

A. Peter

B. James

C. John

D. Andrew

# MARK

LIFE LESSONS: A relationship with Jesus is stronger than any human relationship on earth (3:35).

LIFE LESSONS: Make time for prayer (1:35).

LIFE LESSONS: Faith in Jesus gives believers access to God's healing, transforming power (5:21–43).

## In the Word

This Gospel focuses more on the activities and miracles of Jesus and the reactions of the people rather than on his teachings.

## DID YOU KNOW ?

▶ Only five of the parables Jesus told are documented in the book of Mark.

▶ Throughout the book of Acts and in Paul's letters, Mark is mentioned at various times as ministering with Paul, Barnabas and Silas. He was also a cousin to Barnabas.

## TARGET AUDIENCE

It is generally believed that Mark was targeting the Romans and other Gentiles with his Gospel. He referred to Jesus as the Son of Man 14 times but as the Son of God only 3 times.

## In and Out

*Mark became the subject of a controversy (see Acts 13:13) and caused such a dispute that Paul and Barnabas eventually parted ways for a time (Acts 15:36–41). Paul later requested Mark's company and said, "[Mark] is helpful to me in my ministry" (2 Timothy 4:11), indicating an eventual reconciliation.*

## BY THE NUMBERS

16 CHAPTERS

678 VERSES

13,839 WORDS

# MARK IN REVIEW

 **HOT SEAT**

1. The book of Mark begins with the appearance of John the Baptist in the wilderness. Mark quotes Isaiah's prophecy about the messenger preceding the coming of the Christ, but I also foretold him. Who am I?

**"?" CRYPTIC PHRASES**

2. What was Boanerges?

A. A city Jesus cursed because of lack of faith

B. A name meaning "sons of thunder"

C. The Roman centurion who asked Jesus to heal his servant

D. Another name for the Mount of Olives

 **HOT SEAT**

3. Dealing with all the emotions of my tragedy is so hard, but when I brought it up to Jesus, he told me, "Don't be afraid; just believe." Who am I?

**Q WHO SAID IT?**

4. "Teacher, we saw someone driving out demons in your name and we told him to stop, because he was not one of us."

 **MINUTIAE & MISCELLANY**

5. Which of the following is not the name of one of Jesus' brothers?

A. James

B. John

C. Judas

D. Simon

**TIME TRAVELER**

6. You are Simon of Cyrene, the man chosen to carry Jesus' cross for him. What is the name of your two children?

**Q WHO SAID IT?**

7. "You have heard the blasphemy!"

 **WHERE IN THE WORLD**

8. In the region of the Gerasenes, Jesus drove demons out of a man and into a herd of pigs. The man then went to Decapolis and told people there about Jesus. Which of the following cities, now the capital of Syria, was a part of Decapolis?

A. Joppa

B. Capernaum

C. Damascus

D. Philadelphia

**Q WHO SAID IT?**

9. "Son of David, have mercy on me!"

 **TIME TRAVELER**

10. You tell Jesus that if he is willing, he can heal you. From what do you need healing?

 **MINUTIAE & MISCELLANY**

11. Which group believes there is no resurrection?

A. Sadducees

B. Pharisees

C. Herodians

D. Democrats

 **HOT SEAT**

12. Jesus quotes me when he says, "The sun will be darkened, and the moon will not give its light; the stars will fall from the sky, and the heavenly bodies will be shaken." Who am I?

## What's in a Name?

The name Luke means "luminous" or "light." Both of Luke's books were addressed to someone named Theophilus, whose name means "lover of God" or "friend of God."

# LUKE

## DID YOU KNOW ?

▶ Although divided into fewer chapters, the book of Luke is actually the longest of the four Gospels, having more verses and words than any of the other three. Luke also wrote the book of Acts, and the two books are often considered together as one continuous passage.

▶ Luke was not one of the original 12 apostles, and it is traditionally believed that he was a Gentile.

## In the Word

Luke contains more details regarding the lineage, birth and early years of Jesus than any of the other Gospels. Jesus' family line is documented all the way back to Adam.

## God With Us

Luke highlights both the earthly lineage and the deity of Christ. The phrase Son of Man appears 25 times, and kingdom of God appears 32 times.

### BY THE NUMBERS

24
CHAPTERS

1,151
VERSES

24,180
WORDS

# LUKE IN REVIEW

 **HOT SEAT**

1. I am the father of John the Baptist. What priestly division do I belong to?

 **WHO SAID IT?**

2. "For my eyes have seen your salvation, which you have prepared in the sight of all nations."

 **TIME TRAVELER**

3. You are an 84-year-old widowed prophetess who spends night and day at the temple praying. You are one of the first to see Jesus. What is your father's name?

 **WHO SAID IT?**

4. "Be content with your pay."

 **MINUTIAE & MISCELLANY**

5. While Jesus is being tempted in the desert, he quotes three Old Testament verses. What book do these quotes come from?

 **HOT SEAT**

6. I am the crippled woman that Jesus healed on the Sabbath. How long had I been crippled?

A. 20 years
B. 18 years
C. 30 years
D. 37 years

 **WHO SAID IT?**

7. "We have left all we had to follow you!"

 **TIME TRAVELER**

8. You are the blind beggar who, despite being rebuked, called to Jesus for him to restore your sight. Where are you from?

A. Jericho
B. Jerusalem
C. Damascus
D. Bethlehem

 **WHERE IN THE WORLD**

9. When a complete lack of rain and a great famine lasted for three years and six months in the days of Elijah, God sent Elijah to a widow. In what town did she live?

 **HOT SEAT**

10. I was the governor of Syria about the time of the census that found Mary and Joseph traveling to Bethlehem. Who am I?

A. Pontius Pilate
B. Shealtiel
C. Quirinius
D. Zerubbabel

 **WHO SAID IT?**

11. "My soul glorifies the Lord and my spirit rejoices in God my Savior."

 **MINUTIAE & MISCELLANY**

12. Jesus' followers loudly praised him as he entered Jerusalem on a donkey. This greatly annoyed some of the Pharisees, who asked Jesus to quiet his disciples. But Jesus said that if his disciples kept quiet, something else would "cry out" and praise him. What was he referring to?

A. Birds
B. Stones
C. Buildings of the temple
D. Children

# AUTHOR! AUTHOR!

**John authored five books of the New Testament. Only Paul wrote more books of the New Testament than John.**

# JOHN

## In the Word

▶ In the book of Acts, every time the apostle John is mentioned, he is ministering with Peter.

▶ John referred to God the Father over 100 times and the Holy Spirit over 20 times.

## DID YOU ? KNOW

▶ John was eventually exiled to the island of Patmos, where he was given the vision that became the book of Revelation.

## God With Us

Jesus repeated the phrase "I am" more than 50 times when referring to himself, indicating and reinforcing his deity.

**BY THE NUMBERS**

21 CHAPTERS

879 VERSES

18,614 WORDS

# JOHN IN REVIEW

### Q WHO SAID IT?
1. "Nazareth! Can anything good come from there?"

### 🏆 MINUTIAE & MISCELLANY
2. Were there any Pharisees who didn't believe Jesus was a sinner?

### ⬌ THEN VS. NOW
3. Jesus told a blind man to go wash in the Pool of Siloam. What does Siloam translate to in modern-day English?

### 🏆 MINUTIAE & MISCELLANY
4. How did some of the Jews know that Jesus wasn't a demon?
A. He had opened the eyes of the blind.
B. He had come in peace and wasn't looking for trouble.
C. He had unlikely followers, many of whom were simple fishermen.
D. He said he wasn't a demon.

### 🔥 HOT SEAT
5. I was the first of Jesus' disciples to say that he is the Messiah. Who am I?

### 🏆 MINUTIAE & MISCELLANY
6. What does Jesus say everyone who sins is?

### "?" CRYPTIC PHRASES
7. Illegitimate children
A. They didn't act as their forefathers did.
B. They were adopted Gentiles.
C. Their mother was a prostitute.
D. They didn't register with social security.

### Q WHO SAID IT?
8. "Rabbi, we know that you are a teacher who has come from God. For no one could perform the signs you are doing if God were not with him."

### 🏆 MINUTIAE & MISCELLANY
9. Which of the following does Jesus say he is for the sheep?
A. A grazing field
B. A gate
C. A stream of clean water
D. A doctor

### ✗ WHO DUNNIT?
10. Who plotted to kill Lazarus?

### 🌐 WHERE IN THE WORLD
11. What was the name of the city in Samaria where Jacob's well was located?

### 🏆 MINUTIAE & MISCELLANY
12. Who was Jesus talking about when he prayed, "May they also be in us so that the world may believe that you have sent me"?
A. His disciples
B. The Jews
C. The Gentiles
D. All believers

# DID YOU KNOW ?

▶ The book of Acts begins primarily with the ministry of Peter as the church is established in and near Jerusalem. Then the focus shifts to the missionary journeys centered mostly around Paul and his companions.

# ACTS

## MISSION MINDED

This book does not have a definitive ending, as its works and mission are still proceeding forward to this day.

## In the Word

Numerous occasions are recorded where people became followers of Jesus. On the day of Pentecost, about 3,000 people repented and were baptized (2:41).

## BY THE NUMBERS

28 CHAPTERS

1,007 VERSES

23,109 WORDS

## God With Us

The life of Jesus on earth, which began in the Gospels, was completed in Acts 1 when Jesus ascended into heaven.

# KEY VERSE

"But you will receive power when the Holy Spirit comes on you; and you will be my witnesses in Jerusalem, and in all Judea and Samaria, and to the ends of the earth" (Acts 1:8). This verse was brought to reality through the book of Acts, as the believers first ministered in Jerusalem, then in Samaria and Judea, then on missionary journeys into outer parts of the world.

# ACTS IN REVIEW

## "?" CRYPTIC PHRASES

1. Feeling guilty about betraying Jesus, Judas tried to return the reward money to the chief priests. They didn't want the blood money, so he used it to buy a property where he hung himself. Because of this, the field was called Akeldama. What does that mean?
A. Sinner's land
B. Traitor's place
C. Field of Blood
D. Hill of Guilt

##  HOT SEAT

2. I was the runner-up for the replacement of Judas in the Twelve. Which of the following is not one of my names?
A. Barsabbas
B. James
C. Justus
D. Joseph

##  TIME TRAVELER

3. You are sitting by a gate called Beautiful begging for money because you can't work. Why?

## Q WHO SAID IT?

4. "Leave these men alone! Let them go! For if their purpose or activity is of human origin, it will fail."

## "?" CRYPTIC PHRASES

5. What was Nicanor?
A. A term of contempt used against the people of the Way
B. The name of a believer chosen to feed widows
C. A god of Ephesus
D. An island that rejected the gospel

##  HOT SEAT

6. That was weird. I had just baptized a eunuch after explaining to him a passage in Isaiah and telling him how it had been fulfilled through Jesus. Suddenly, BOOM! I found myself no longer waist deep in water but in a city called Azotus. It was so puzzling! Who am I?

## "?" CRYPTIC PHRASES

7. What was the Synagogue of the Freedmen?
A. The church of Christians of Antioch
B. A place for Jews of Cyrene, Alexandria, Cilicia and Asia
C. A common place for Saul to grab people of the Way
D. A church in Athens for worshipers of the god Greca

##  TIME TRAVELER

8. You are before the Sanhedrin, and you give an account of the beginning of Israel from Abraham to Moses to Solomon. Who are you?

##  WHO DUNNIT?

9. Who tried to buy the power of the Holy Spirit from the apostles but was then rebuked by Peter because he thought he could do so?

## Q WHO SAID IT?

10. "I will give you the holy and sure blessings promised to David." Whom does Paul quote here?

##  MINUTIAE & MISCELLANY

11. Who went to Achaia to preach the gospel and won a debate with local Jews about whether or not Jesus was the Messiah prophesied in the Scriptures?

##  TIME TRAVELER

12. You insulted Ananias by calling him a "whitewashed wall." You didn't realize, though, that Ananias was the high priest, so you didn't intentionally break the law from Exodus that says not to speak evil about the ruler of your people. Who are you?
A. Paul
B. Peter
C. Barnabas
D. Caesar

# ROMANS
## KEY VERSE

*"If you declare with your mouth, 'Jesus is Lord,' and believe in your heart that God raised him from the dead, you will be saved" (10:9).*

LIFE LESSONS: When you judge others, you are really condemning yourself (2:1).

LIFE LESSONS: Faith in Jesus saves people from sin (3:21-24). Be careful not to slow others' spiritual growth (14:13).

## BY THE NUMBERS

**16** CHAPTERS

**433** VERSES

**9,880** WORDS

## WHEN IN ROME

Historians calculate that at the time of Paul's writing, Rome had a population of over four million. It was the capital of the Roman Empire and included some of the most impressive structures and features of its time. The book of Romans was written to the growing church in Rome to equip the believers for evangelism and discipleship.

## DID YOU ? KNOW

▶ The book of Romans is sometimes called "The Gospel According to Paul."

▶ The book of Acts records Paul as a prisoner in Rome, awaiting an audience with Caesar and other prominent leaders of the Roman Empire.

## In the Word

The word sin (or transgression or trespass) appears over 70 times. The word righteous (or righteousness) appears 45 times; mercy appears 14 times; holy appears 14 times; faith (or faithfulness) appears 42 times.

# ROMANS IN REVIEW

 **MINUTIAE & MISCELLANY**
1. What does Paul say he delights in?

**Q WHO SAID IT?**
2. "So that you may be proved right when you speak and prevail when you judge."

A. Isaiah

B. Hosea

C. David

D. Micah

 **MINUTIAE & MISCELLANY**
3. What does Paul say we will also do if we die with Christ?

 **TIME TRAVELER**
4. You are the one who wrote the letter at Paul's diction. Who are you?

 **MINUTIAE & MISCELLANY**
5. "At the present time, there is a remnant chosen by grace. And if by grace, then it cannot be based on _____." (Fill in the blank.)

**Q WHO SAID IT?**
6. "Who has known the mind of the Lord? Or who has been his counselor?" Which prophet does Paul quote?

 **MINUTIAE & MISCELLANY**
7. What does Paul tell us never to be lacking in?

A. Courage

B. Faith

C. Zeal

D. Sleep

 **HOT SEAT**
8. Paul quoted me by saying, "The righteous will live by faith." Who am I?

 **HOT SEAT**
9. What does Paul compare the Gentiles to in Romans 11?

A. Newborn children in need of proper nourishment

B. Weeping willows blowing in the breeze

C. Ripened figs waiting to be picked

D. Grafted branches on an olive tree

 **TIME TRAVELER**
10. You are the man whose mother Paul said had been a mother to him too. Who are you?

**"?" CRYPTIC PHRASES**
11. What phrase does Paul write that was used to describe the full legal standing of an adopted heir in Roman culture?

A. Adoption to sonship

B. Becoming of princeship

C. Acceptance of successorship

D. Deriving of stance

 **MINUTIAE & MISCELLANY**
12. According to Paul, "Everything that does not come from faith is _____."
(Fill in the blank.)

# 1 CORINTHIANS

## INTERSECTION

Historians record that at the time of this writing, the city of Corinth was the capital of the Roman province of Achaia. It had a population of around 700,000 and was the site of many temples to false gods.

## GROWING UP

*Topics Specific to Church Growth*

Sexual purity *(7:1–40)*

Spiritual purity *(8:1–10:33)*

Communion *(11:17–34)*

Spiritual gifts *(chapters 12 and 14)*

God's love *(chapter 13)*

Orderly worship *(14:26–40)*

The resurrection *(chapter 15)*

## LOVING IT

One of the most popular passages of Scripture, known as the "Love Chapter," is 1 Corinthians 13.

## In the Word

The church at Corinth had so many problems that Paul dedicated the first six chapters of his letter to addressing the issues of divisions in the church, people's foolishness and God's wisdom, spiritual maturity, worship of human leaders, sexual immorality and lawsuits among believers. Chapter 7 then begins with "Now for the matters you wrote about . . ."

## BY THE NUMBERS

16 CHAPTERS

437 VERSES

9,721 WORDS

## DID YOU KNOW ?

▶ In spite of facing rejection in the synagogue and other opposition, Paul stayed in Corinth a year and a half, preaching the Word and building up the body of believers.

# 1 CORINTHIANS IN REVIEW

 **MINUTIAE & MISCELLANY**

1. What does Paul say God exposes?

A. Backstabbers and blind guides

B. Motives of the heart

C. Fools who think they are wise

D. False prophets

 **HOT SEAT**

2. I co-wrote the book of 1 Corinthians with Paul. Who am I?

 **MINUTIAE & MISCELLANY**

3. What does Paul say the message of the cross is to those who are perishing?

A. Misunderstood knowledge

B. Unattainable wisdom

C. Foolishness

D. Judgment

**Q WHO SAID IT?**

4. "Who has known the mind of the Lord so as to instruct him?" Who is Paul quoting?

 **MINUTIAE & MISCELLANY**

5. What does Paul say God has done to the wisdom of the world?

 **TIME TRAVELER**

6. You are the person Paul quotes when he says, "The earth is the Lord's, and everything in it." Who are you?

 **MINUTIAE & MISCELLANY**

7. Who does Paul say the gift of speaking in tongues is a sign to?

A. Unbelievers

B. The Holy Spirit

C. The angels

D. Fellow believers

 **HOT SEAT**

8. I don't understand it! When I speak in the tongues of men and angels, I only sound like a resounding gong or a clanging symbol. What am I missing?

 **MINUTIAE & MISCELLANY**

9. Where does Paul say he was going before he would go to Corinth?

 **WHO DUNNIT?**

10. Who at first was unwilling to go to Corinth but was persuaded by Paul to do so?

 **MINUTIAE & MISCELLANY**

11. "Do everything in _____."
(Fill in the blank.)

 **TIME TRAVELER**

12. You and your wife told Paul to send your greetings to the church in Corinth. Who are you?

A. Apollos

B. Aquila

C. Peter

D. Barnabas

## In the Word

Because of outside opposition to his preaching, Paul spoke out in defense of his own ministry through three entire chapters of this book (*chapters 10–12*).

# 2 CORINTHIANS
# KEY VERSES

*"For our light and momentary troubles are achieving for us an eternal glory that far outweighs them all" (4:17).*

*"My grace is sufficient for you, for my power is made perfect in weakness" (12:9).*

*"Do not be yoked together with unbelievers" (6:14).*

*"Now he who supplies seed to the sower and bread for food will also supply and increase your store of seed and will enlarge the harvest of your righteousness" (9:10).*

*"Therefore, if anyone is in Christ, the new creation has come: The old has gone, the new is here" (5:17)!*

*"Now the Lord is the Spirit, and where the Spirit of the Lord is, there is freedom" (3:17).*

## BY THE NUMBERS

13 CHAPTERS

257 VERSES

6,247 WORDS

## SOWING AND REAPING

Chapters 8 and 9 provide the most detailed teachings of generosity, financial giving and ministry support in the New Testament.

## DID YOU KNOW ?

▶ This letter is addressed to the church in Corinth, as well as to believers throughout the province of Achaia, of which Corinth was the capital city.

# 2 CORINTHIANS IN REVIEW

**⏱ TIME TRAVELER**
1. You co-wrote the book of 2 Corinthians with Paul. Who are you?

**⭐ MINUTIAE & MISCELLANY**
2. What Old Testament book did Paul quote when he accredited God as saying, "I will be a Father to you, and you will be my sons and daughters"?

**"?" CRYPTIC PHRASES**
3. What was Silvanus?
A. A river that flowed through Macedonia
B. An island Paul was to pass through on his way to Corinth
C. A name for Silas (in Greek)
D. A country that John had been exiled to near the island of Patmos

**⭐ MINUTIAE & MISCELLANY**
4. Where did Paul go but had no peace of mind because Titus wasn't there as he'd expected?
A. Rome
B. The island of Crete
C. Troas
D. Timothy's house

**Q WHO SAID IT?**
5. "Let the one who boasts boast in the Lord." Who does Paul quote here?

**⭐ MINUTIAE & MISCELLANY**
6. Where does Paul say we have treasures to show that all-surpassing power is from God and not from us?

**🔥 HOT SEAT**
7. I was the king of Syria who had the governor of Damascus guard the city of Damascenes in order to arrest Paul. Who am I?

**⭐ MINUTIAE & MISCELLANY**
8. How many times does Paul say he had received the "forty lashes minus one"?

**Q WHO SAID IT?**
9. "In the time of my favor I heard you, and in the day of salvation I helped you." From what book is Paul quoting?

**🔥 HOT SEAT**
10. I am what God allowed to remain in Paul to keep him from becoming conceited. What am I?

**Q WHO SAID IT?**
11. "Every matter must be established by the testimony of two or three witnesses." Who is Paul quoting when he says this?

**⭐ MINUTIAE & MISCELLANY**
12. What does Paul say is achieving for us an eternal glory?
A. Our light and momentary troubles
B. Our kindness toward our neighbors
C. Our ability to preach the gospel
D. Our patience with our children

# KEY PASSAGE

*"But the fruit of the Spirit is love, joy, peace, forbearance, kindness, goodness, faithfulness, gentleness and self-control" (5:22–23).*

# GALATIANS

## DID YOU? KNOW

▶ The book of Galatians was written "to the churches in Galatia" *(1:2)*, indicating not one specific congregation but a number of churches in a large region. All these churches were under similar pressures from outsiders to change their beliefs, which caused confusion in their meetings.

## In the Word

In the book of Galatians, believers are taught to leave the bondage of sin and law to find freedom through faith in the grace of God and in the Holy Spirit. In the six chapters of the book of Galatians, the word law appears 34 times; grace appears 8 times; faith appears 21 times; and references to the Holy Spirit appear 18 times.

## ON THE GO

Although Paul traveled extensively to new regions and territories spreading the gospel, he still took time to write letters of instruction and encouragement to the churches and individuals he had ministered to previously.

## FOLLOW MY LEAD

Chapter 2 gives the account of Paul's confrontation with Peter as an example to inspire the churches to resist erroneous teaching and traditions.

**BY THE NUMBERS**

6
CHAPTERS

149
VERSES

3,243
WORDS

LIFE LESSONS: Seek God's approval, not the approval of people (1:10). Address sinful behavior (2:11–14).

LIFE LESSONS: The fruit of the Spirit is evidence of God's power and work in you (5:22–23).

# GALATIANS IN REVIEW

 **MINUTIAE & MISCELLANY**

1. What did the Galatians do that astonished Paul?

A. *They had welcomed him back into their fellowship.*

B. *They had quickly deserted the gospel.*

C. *They had collected a large amount of money for Paul.*

D. *They had all disappeared.*

**WHO DUNNIT?**

2. Which apostle does Paul reprimand for leading several believers astray by choosing to separate himself from Gentiles in Antioch?

 **MINUTIAE & MISCELLANY**

3. "God does not show _____." (Fill in the blank.)

**HOT SEAT**

4. I am Moses. Which of the books attributed to me does Paul quote when he writes, "The slave woman's son will never share in the inheritance with the free woman's son"?

**MINUTIAE & MISCELLANY**

5. What does Paul say we do if we say we're something we're not?

**MINUTIAE & MISCELLANY**

6. Paul encourages the Galatians to stand firm, and he warns them not to become burdened by something. What is it?

A. *A yoke of unbelief*

B. *A yoke of idolatry*

C. *A yoke of oxen*

D. *A yoke of slavery*

 **MINUTIAE & MISCELLANY**

7. What does Paul say was our guardian until Christ came?

A. *The angels*

B. *The Holy Spirit*

C. *The law*

D. *The priests*

 **HOT SEAT**

8. I'm Hagar. What Biblical landmark do I represent, according to Galatians?

 **MINUTIAE & MISCELLANY**

9. "Now you, brothers and sisters, like Isaac, are _____." (Fill in the blank.)

A. *Children of promise*

B. *Spared from the knife*

C. *Offspring of Abraham*

D. *Destined for greatness*

 **TIME TRAVELER**

10. Paul says you should be "under God's curse." What could you have done to earn this derisive implication?

A. *Believed the deception of a false prophet*

B. *Tried to preach another gospel than that of Christ*

C. *Refused to show hospitality to God's chosen messenger*

D. *Ate the fruit from a forbidden tree*

 **MINUTIAE & MISCELLANY**

11. What does Paul say was the very thing he was eager to do that James, John and Peter told him to do?

**HOT SEAT**

12. You and Peter were the only two apostles Paul saw when he first stayed in Jerusalem three years after his conversion. Who are you?

## Following Up

Paul wrote this letter to the church in Ephesus, where he had spent over two years preaching and arguing the gospel in both the synagogue and in other meeting locations.

**6** CHAPTERS
**155** VERSES
**3,077** WORDS

# EPHESIANS

## AUTHOR! AUTHOR!

**Paul wrote this book while chained in prison for his preaching and mission.**

## UP IN SMOKE

New believers in Ephesus who previously practiced sorcery publicly burned their scrolls, collectively valued at over 50,000 days' wages (see Acts 19:19).

## MIRACLES!

*The church in Ephesus experienced many miracles such as recorded in Acts 19:11–12: "God did extraordinary miracles through Paul, so that even handkerchiefs and aprons that had touched him were taken to the sick, and their illnesses were cured and the evil spirits left them."*

## In the Word

Paul followed a theme of supernatural power and spiritual warfare for victorious believers, referencing the word heaven nine times.

# EPHESIANS IN REVIEW

## ⭐ MINUTIAE & MISCELLANY
1. What does Paul say is the seal with which we were marked in Christ?

A. *The blood of Christ*

B. *The title Christian*

C. *The Holy Spirit*

D. *The knowledge from the Word of God*

## Q WHO SAID IT?
2. "In your anger do not sin." Who originally said this?

## ⭐ MINUTIAE & MISCELLANY
3. What did God prepare "in advance for us to do"?

## ⭐ MINUTIAE & MISCELLANY
4. Paul says he has not stopped praying for the Ephesians. What does he keep asking God for so they would know God better?

A. *Peace in their suffering*

B. *The Spirit of wisdom and revelation*

C. *Forgiveness*

D. *Faith*

## ⭐ MINUTIAE & MISCELLANY
5. What does Paul say we should give thanks to God for in Ephesians 5:20?

## ⏱ TIME TRAVELER
6. You are what Paul asks the Ephesians not to be discouraged about. What are you?

A. *A false prophet*

B. *The crumbling temple walls*

C. *Unbelieving ears*

D. *Paul's suffering*

## 🔥 HOT SEAT
7. I am Paul. What do I describe as "less than the least of all the Lord's people"?

A. *Satan among angels*

B. *Myself (Paul)*

C. *He who discriminates against the Gentiles*

D. *He who proclaims Christ with his mouth yet denies him by his works*

## ⭐ MINUTIAE & MISCELLANY
8. "When he ascended on high, he took many captives and gave gifts to his people." What book does this quote originally come from?

## 🏹 WHO DUNNIT?
9. According to Paul, what people have "lost all sensitivity"?

## ⭐ MINUTIAE & MISCELLANY
10. What does Paul say there should be instead of "obscenity, foolish talk or coarse joking, which are out of place"?

## ⏱ TIME TRAVELER
11. At the end of his book, Paul said he would send you to the Ephesians. Who are you?

## ⭐ MINUTIAE & MISCELLANY
12. Paul says not to be partners with those who _____.
(Fill in the blank.)

A. *Refuse to show you hospitality*

B. *Are disobedient*

C. *Keep secrets*

D. *Refuse to sing*

# What's in a Name?

Paul wrote to the church in the city of Philippi, which got its name from King Philip of Macedonia, the father of Alexander the Great.

# PHILIPPIANS

## AUTHOR! AUTHOR!

Although traditionally Paul has been considered the author, Philippians is addressed to the church as from both Paul and Timothy. It becomes clear through the text, however, that the author is indeed Paul.

*LOOKING UP*

In spite of his prison chains, Paul wrote this book with a theme of joyfulness, using the word joy (or rejoice) 13 times.

## DID YOU KNOW?

**BY THE NUMBERS**

4 CHAPTERS

104 VERSES

2,294 WORDS

▶ Paul originally arrived in Philippi as a result of a dream he had been given, where a man from Macedonia spoke to him, saying, "Come over to Macedonia and help us" *(Acts 16:9).* Paul immediately left Troas and went to Philippi, a leading city of that region of Macedonia.

# KEY PASSAGE

"Rejoice in the Lord always. I will say it again: Rejoice! Let your gentleness be evident to all. The Lord is near. Do not be anxious about anything, but in every situation, by prayer and petition, with thanksgiving, present your requests to God. And the peace of God, which transcends all understanding, will guard your hearts and your minds in Christ Jesus *(4:4–7)."*

# PHILIPPIANS IN REVIEW

## Q WHO SAID IT?

1. Paul said that we are to be "children of God without fault in a warped and crooked generation," which is a quote from an Old Testament book. Who originally said it?

##  MINUTIAE & MISCELLANY

2. What does Paul say he did every time he remembered God's people in Philippi?

A. Grieved

B. Fasted for a day

C. Thanked God

D. Rejoiced

## ⏱ TIME TRAVELER

3. Paul says you were ill and almost died but then God had mercy on you. Who are you?

A. Epaphroditus

B. Timothy

C. Silas

D. Demas

##  MINUTIAE & MISCELLANY

4. How many times does Paul quote the Old Testament in the book of Philippians?

## "?" CRYPTIC PHRASES

5. What is Syntyche?

A. Name of a woman who Paul pleads with to be of the same mind

B. The lake from which the guards got the water for the prisoners

C. The doctrine of the Roman religion that Paul denounces in chapter 5

D. A guard who had converted to Christianity

##  MINUTIAE & MISCELLANY

6. What did Paul say had become "clear throughout the whole palace guard"?

A. That Paul appeared to be a fool

B. That Paul was in chains for Christ

C. That Paul was severely lacking in nutrition

D. That Paul's presence brought unexplainable peace to them

## 🔥 HOT SEAT

7. Paul describes me as one who will show "genuine concern" for the believers' welfare. Who am I?

##  MINUTIAE & MISCELLANY

8. What does Paul say we should "live up to"?

A. What we've already attained

B. What God has shown us through the Philippian church

C. What our ancestors have done before us

D. What Paul expects for church attendance

## "?" CRYPTIC PHRASES

9. Who is Paul talking about when he says, "Their god is their stomach"?

##  MINUTIAE & MISCELLANY

10. What does Paul say we should make "evident to all"?

## ⏱ TIME TRAVELER

11. God's people in your household sent greetings to the Philippians through Paul's letter. Who are you?

##  MINUTIAE & MISCELLANY

12. What does Paul say we should do with everything we have heard, learned or received from him?

# KEY PASSAGE

"So then, just as you received Christ Jesus as Lord, continue to live your lives in him, rooted and built up in him, strengthened in the faith as you were taught, and overflowing with thankfulness" *(2:6-7)*.

## PASS IT ON

This letter from Paul was written to the Colossians, but it was also to be read to the church at Laodicea *(4:16)*.

## FREEDOM BOUND

Paul wrote this letter while chained in prison, yet he asked for prayer that he would continue to proclaim Christ clearly even though he was persecuted for doing so.

# COLOSSIANS

## In Christ

Believers are taught to focus on Jesus Christ, the Son of God. In this short book, the words Jesus, Christ or God appear over 65 times.

# DID YOU ? KNOW

▶ This book was written by Paul to the church in Colossae, a city in Phrygia, in Roman territory, located about 120 miles east of Ephesus in the Lycus River Valley, near the foot of Mount Cadmus.

## BY THE NUMBERS

4 CHAPTERS

95 VERSES

2,069 WORDS

# TITUS

LIFE LESSONS: Confront false teachers who try to warp God's truth (1:10-14).

LIFE LESSONS: Treat others with goodness and love, as Jesus has done for you (3:3-8). Be self-controlled (2:6-8).

## DID YOU KNOW ?

▶ Titus is mentioned 14 times in Paul's letters, but never in the book of Acts.

▶ Titus—like Timothy, Barnabas, Luke and many others—served alongside Paul in his missionary travels and often went on solo journeys to teach and encourage the various churches. Paul referred to Titus as his partner and coworker among the believers.

## REACHING OUT

Paul had entrusted Titus with continuing the ministry on the island of Crete, in the Mediterranean Sea (1:5). The island, which is about 170 miles long and 30 miles wide, was populated with characters of bad reputation.

### In the Word

Titus, like Timothy, was a minister under Paul's leadership. His book also bears similarities to the books written to Timothy, containing instructions and teachings for personal ministry as well as church growth and development.

## KEY PASSAGE

"For the grace of God has appeared that offers salvation to all people. It teaches us to say 'No' to ungodliness and worldly passions, and to live self-controlled, upright and godly lives in this present age, while we wait for the blessed hope—the appearing of the glory of our great God and Savior, Jesus Christ" (2:11-13).

# TITUS IN REVIEW

 **MINUTIAE & MISCELLANY**
1. What does Paul say an elder must be?

 **HOT SEAT**
2. I am the Cretan philosopher who Paul quotes when he says, "Cretans are always liars, evil brutes, lazy gluttons." Who am I?

 **MINUTIAE & MISCELLANY**
3. Where does Paul ask Titus to meet him?

 **MINUTIAE & MISCELLANY**
4. What does Paul encourage the young men to be?
A. Courageous
B. Selfless
C. Self-controlled
D. Full of wisdom

 **MINUTIAE & MISCELLANY**
5. What does Paul say we should do with all authority?

 **TIME TRAVELER**
6. You are a divisive person. How many times does Paul say you will be warned?
A. Only once
B. Twice
C. Three times
D. As many times as needed

# PHILEMON IN REVIEW

 **HOT SEAT**
1. I am Philemon. What does Paul say I owe him?

 **MINUTIAE & MISCELLANY**
2. Who of the following isn't specified as having sent their greetings?
A. Mark
B. Luke
C. Demas
D. Barnabas

 **TIME TRAVELER**
3. You co-write the book of Philemon with Paul. Who are you?

 **MINUTIAE & MISCELLANY**
4. Which of the following does Paul specifically use to describe himself in this book?
A. An old man
B. A temple leader
C. A high-ranking Sadducee
D. Biblical authority

 **HOT SEAT**
5. Paul calls me a fellow soldier. Who am I?
A. Apphia
B. Archippus
C. Aristarchus
D. Acridos

 **MINUTIAE & MISCELLANY**
6. What does Paul say has given him great joy and encouragement?

# KEY PASSAGE

"I always thank my God as I remember you in my prayers, because I hear about your love for all his holy people and your faith in the Lord Jesus" *(verses 4-5).*

# PHILEMON

LIFE LESSONS: Loving and serving others influences lives (verse 7).

LIFE LESSONS: Forgive as God has forgiven you (verses 17–19).

## In the Word

This book revolves primarily around a man named Onesimus, who appears to have been a slave owned by Philemon but had recently become converted by Paul. In this letter, Paul explained the change and asked Philemon to accept Onesimus no longer as a slave but as a brother in the Lord.

## Bondage to FREEDOM

Paul wrote the letter to Philemon while he was chained in a Roman prison, where he had recently prayed with Onesimus the slave to receive Christ and be free from sin.

### GREETINGS!

Paul wrote this letter not only to Philemon but also to the church that met in his home and to two other believers, Apphia and Archippus.

## DID YOU ? KNOW

▶ This letter is the shortest written by Paul, containing only 25 verses.

## BY THE NUMBERS

1 CHAPTER

25 VERSES

480 WORDS

# HEBREWS

## BRINGING IT FORWARD
Connections and parallels between the Old and New Testaments:

Speaking through the prophets vs. Jesus (1:1–2:18)

Moses vs. Jesus (3:1-19)

Sabbath-rest (4:1-11)

Jesus the high priest (4:14–8:13)

The tabernacle (9:1-28)

Christ the sacrifice (10:1-39)

## BY THE NUMBERS

13 CHAPTERS

303 VERSES

7,048 WORDS

## DID YOU KNOW?

▶ The author of the book of Hebrews is unknown, although some scholars believe it could have been Paul.

▶ Hebrews contains more than 40 direct quotes from the Old Testament.

## In the Word
This book is presented as a legal argument to the Jews, to prove that Jesus is the Christ, the fulfillment of the law.

## FAITH PARADE
One of the most popular chapters in the Bible, called the "Hall of Faith" or the "Faith Chapter," is Hebrews 11.

LIFE LESSONS: Those who trust Christ are his brothers and sisters (2:11–12). Commit to Jesus (5:13–14).

LIFE LESSONS: Jesus, being fully human and fully God, relates to your temptations and struggles (4:15).

# HEBREWS IN REVIEW

##  WHO SAID IT?

1. "For I will forgive their wickedness and will remember their sins no more." Who did the author quote here?

##  MINUTIAE & MISCELLANY

2. What does the author say the old covenant had become?

A. Lost

B. Unimportant

C. Forgotten

D. Inferior

##  TIME TRAVELER

3. The author said you are a "ministering spirit sent to serve those who will inherit salvation." What are you?

## MINUTIAE & MISCELLANY

4. What does the author say we must pay the most careful attention to?

A. The signs of the times

B. The message of salvation we have heard

C. The false prophets

D. The voices of the angels singing in unison

##  HOT SEAT

5. I originally said, "What is mankind that you are mindful of them, a son of man that you care for him?" Who am I?

## MINUTIAE & MISCELLANY

6. "But encourage one another daily, as long as it is called _____."
(Fill in the blank.)

##  WHERE IN THE WORLD

7. The author tells the Hebrews that the believers in a country still standing today sent their greetings to them. Which country?

##  MINUTIAE & MISCELLANY

8. The author quotes Psalm 95: "Do not harden your hearts as you did in the rebellion." In the original psalm, the name of a place, Meribah, is given as an example of what we are not to do. What does the name Meribah mean?

A. Gossiping

B. Quarreling

C. Deceiving

D. Unsharing

##  TIME TRAVELER

9. You are the priest and king of Salem that Jesus is compared to. Who are you?

##  MINUTIAE & MISCELLANY

10. We are told by the author of Hebrews not "to become _____, but to imitate those who through faith and patience inherit what has been promised."
(Fill in the blank.)

##  TIME TRAVELER

11. There are two people who, according to the Bible, never died. You are the one whose faith is commended in Hebrews.
Who are you?

## MINUTIAE & MISCELLANY

12. The author tells us not to be godless, and he gives us an example from the Old Testament. Whose godlessness is mentioned?

A. Achan's

B. Korah's

C. Esau's

D. Ahab's

# AUTHOR! AUTHOR!

Most scholars agree that the author is James the brother of Jesus, since the apostle James would have died before it was written. James may not have been a believer until after the resurrection and eventually became a leader in the church.

## BY THE NUMBERS

5 CHAPTERS

108 VERSES

2,316 WORDS

## In the Word

Believers are called to put their faith into action. The word faith appears 14 times; the words do, deeds or action appear 31 times.

## DID YOU KNOW ?

▶ This book is addressed to the 12 tribes of Israel scattered among the nations.

# JAMES

## LOOKING BACK

Even though this book has only five chapters, it contains seven direct quotes from the Old Testament.

# KEY PASSAGE

"Do not merely listen to the word, and so deceive yourselves. Do what it says. Anyone who listens to the word but does not do what it says is like someone who looks at his face in a mirror and, after looking at himself, goes away and immediately forgets what he looks like. But whoever looks intently into the perfect law that gives freedom, and continues in it—not forgetting what they have heard, but doing it—they will be blessed in what they do" (1:22-25).

# JAMES IN REVIEW

 **MINUTIAE & MISCELLANY**

1. What does James say everyone should be quick to do?

 **MINUTIAE & MISCELLANY**

2. What does James say doesn't produce the righteousness God desires?

 **WHO SAID IT?**

3. "God opposes the proud but shows favor to the humble." Who originally said this?

 **MINUTIAE & MISCELLANY**

4. What does James say "believers in our glorious Lord Jesus Christ must not" do?

A. *Show favoritism*

B. *Deceive children*

C. *Speak falsely*

D. *Gossip*

 **TIME TRAVELER**

5. You are what James says triumphs over judgment. What are you?

 **MINUTIAE & MISCELLANY**

6. According to James, what should we show by our good life?

A. *Integrity and honesty*

B. *Good works that outweigh our evil deeds*

C. *Wisdom and understanding*

D. *Mastery of speech*

 **HOT SEAT**

7. James uses the rudder of a ship as an example of me. What am I?

 **MINUTIAE & MISCELLANY**

8. What does James say the peacemakers, who sow peace, reap?

 **TIME TRAVELER**

9. You are what James compares life to. What are you?

A. *Grass*

B. *Fire*

C. *Mist*

D. *Smoke*

ANSWERS:
1. listen (1:19) 2. human anger (1:20) 3. Solomon (4:6; see Proverbs 3:34) 4. A (2:1) 5. mercy (2:13) 6. C (3:13) 7. tongue (3:4–5) 8. righteousness (3:18) 9. C (4:14)

# 1 PETER

## What's in a Name?

The name Peter (or Petros) means "Rock."

## STANDING STRONG

Peter encouraged believers to stay strong in their faith during trials and persecution, referencing the word suffer (or suffering) 18 times.

### ON THE ROCK

Peter, a Jew, was an original leader of the church in Jerusalem. His book appeals to the Jews to accept and stand for Jesus. Peter quoted 12 specific passages from the Old Testament in his appeal.

## KEY PASSAGE

"For you know that it was not with perishable things such as silver or gold that you were redeemed from the empty way of life handed down to you from your ancestors, but with the precious blood of Christ, a lamb without blemish or defect" *(1:18-19)*.

## BY THE NUMBERS

5
CHAPTERS

105
VERSES

2,495
WORDS

## REACHING OUT

Peter wrote to believers scattered throughout the provinces of Pontus, Galatia, Cappadocia, Asia and Bithynia *(1:1)*.

LIFE LESSONS: Live a God-honoring life that draws unbelievers toward God (2:12).

LIFE LESSONS: The world watches how you respond to and obey authority (2:13-15). Rejoice when you experience suffering because of your faith (4:14).

# 1 PETER IN REVIEW

### "?" CRYPTIC PHRASES
1. What does Peter mean by "pure spiritual milk"?

A. *The headwaters of Euphrates*

B. *Clean water for missionaries*

C. *Feeding on the Word of God*

D. *The vision of the river flowing in heaven*

### Q WHO SAID IT?
2. "All people are like grass, and all their glory is like the flowers of the field; the grass withers and the flowers fall, but the word of the Lord endures forever." Which prophet does Peter quote?

### MINUTIAE & MISCELLANY
3. What does Peter say we should do "without grumbling"?

A. *Offer hospitality to one another*

B. *Speak the truth in love*

C. *Share our possessions with one another*

D. *Pray and fast*

### TIME TRAVELER
4. Peter refers to you as his son. Who are you?

### Q WHO SAID IT?
5. "For the eyes of the Lord are on the righteous and his ears are attentive to their prayer." Who originally said this?

### HOT SEAT
6. I am what the water that saved Noah and his family represents to believers. What am I?

# 2 PETER IN REVIEW

### HOT SEAT
1. I am the one Peter says "was tormented in his righteous soul by the lawless deeds he saw and heard." Who am I?

### MINUTIAE & MISCELLANY
2. Peter quotes God, saying, "This is my Son, whom I love; with him I am well pleased." When did Peter say he heard God say it?

A. *During Jesus' baptism*

B. *During the transfiguration on the sacred mountain*

C. *During the Last Supper before the crucifixion*

D. *During the moments just before Jesus' ascension*

### TIME TRAVELER
3. You are what Peter says will come like a thief. What are you?

### MINUTIAE & MISCELLANY
4. What has Jesus' divine power given us?

### HOT SEAT
5. I am what Peter says the present earth and heavens are being reserved for. What am I?

### MINUTIAE & MISCELLANY
6. What did Peter say he thought was right to do?

A. *Refresh his readers' memories*

B. *Point out his readers' faults*

C. *Share his belongings with his readers*

D. *Visit his readers as soon as possible*

## In the Word

Peter stated the purpose of his two letters: (1) to stimulate wholesome thinking; (2) to recall the words of the prophets; and (3) to recall the Lord's command given through the apostles *(3:1–2)*.

# 2 PETER

## GIVING IT ALL

*Historians record that Peter was crucified under order of Roman emperor Nero, who had announced himself as an enemy of God and slaughtered many Christians, including Paul. It is also traditionally believed that Peter was crucified upside down, because he stated that he was "unworthy to die in the same manner as [his] Lord."*

## Reaching Beyond

This letter from Peter is addressed to all believers, "those who through the righteousness of our God and Savior Jesus Christ have received a faith as precious as ours" *(1:1)*.

## DID YOU KNOW ?

▶ This book had at least three authors, including Solomon, Agur and Lemuel.

## BY THE NUMBERS

3
CHAPTERS

61
VERSES

1,552
WORDS

# KEY PASSAGE

"His divine power has given us everything we need for a godly life through our knowledge of him who called us by his own glory and goodness. Through these he has given us his very great and precious promises, so that through them you may participate in the divine nature, having escaped the corruption in the world caused by evil desires *(1:3–4)*."

## Worth Repeating

In this letter, John repeated the popular message found in his Gospel: "This is how God showed his love among us: He sent his one and only Son into the world that we might live through him" *(4:9; see John 3:16).*

BY THE NUMBERS

**5**
CHAPTERS

**105**
VERSES

**2,525**
WORDS

# 1 JOHN

# KEY VERSE

"God is love. Whoever lives in love lives in God, and God in them" (4:16).

## Did You See That?

John began his testimony by appealing to human senses: "That which was from the beginning, which we have heard, which we have seen with our eyes, which we have looked at and our hands have touched—this we proclaim concerning the Word of life" *(1:1).*

## Life in Christ

John wrote about eternal life in Christ, referring to the word life 15 times.

### LOVE LETTER

John emphasized seeking God's love and turning from the world. References to God together with the word love appear in 21 verses.

LIFE LESSONS: Actions speak more about your character than words (1:6). Sincerely confess sin to God (1:9).

LIFE LESSONS: The Bible truthfully and accurately reveals God and the things of God (4:1).

# 1 JOHN IN REVIEW

 **MINUTIAE & MISCELLANY**

1. Which of the following does John not say about those who claim to be without sin?

A. *They deceive themselves.*

B. *They make God out to be a liar.*

C. *They sin by saying they are sinless.*

D. *The truth isn't in them.*

 **HOT SEAT**

2. I am what John says sin is. What am I?

 **MINUTIAE & MISCELLANY**

3. What does John say all who hope in Christ do?

A. *Walk blamelessly*

B. *Speak the truth in love*

C. *Purify themselves*

D. *Reject false teachings*

 **TIME TRAVELER**

4. You are the reason we know that we live in God and he in us. What are you?

 **MINUTIAE & MISCELLANY**

5. What is the last command in 1 John?

# 3 JOHN IN REVIEW

 **MINUTIAE & MISCELLANY**

1. What does John say we ought to do?

 **MINUTIAE & MISCELLANY**

2. Who is "well spoken of by everyone—and even by the truth itself"?

A. *Demetrius*

B. *Diotrephes*

C. *Gaius*

D. *John*

 **TIME TRAVELER**

3. You are Diotrephes. What does John say you love?

A. *To be first*

B. *To keep quiet*

C. *To gossip*

D. *To hide*

 **MINUTIAE & MISCELLANY**

4. What is the last thing John says to do in the final greetings?

 **HOT SEAT**

5. I am what John refers to himself as. What am I?

A. *The father*

B. *The teacher*

C. *The elder*

D. *The messenger*

# 2 JOHN IN REVIEW

 **TIME TRAVELER**

1. You are God's command from the beginning. What are you?

A. *Walk in love.*

B. *Walk in the truth.*

C. *Walk in wisdom and understanding.*

D. *Walk in peace.*

 **MINUTIAE & MISCELLANY**

2. "Whoever continues in the teaching [of Christ] has both the _____ and the _____." (Fill in the blanks.)

 **HOT SEAT**

3. I am what John says anyone who doesn't acknowledge that Jesus came in the flesh is. What am I?

# AUTHOR! AUTHOR!

John wrote five books of the New Testament: his Gospel, three letters and Revelation. Only Paul wrote more.

# 2 JOHN

LIFE LESSONS: *Don't trust teaching that contradicts the Bible (verse 7).*

LIFE LESSONS: *Don't support wicked, false teachers or false religions (verse 11).*

## BELIEVERS VS. DECEIVERS

John included in this letter both encouragement for believers *(verse 4)* and warnings against deceivers *(verse 7).*

# DID YOU ? KNOW

▶ John and his brother James were among the first disciples called by Jesus to follow him. Jesus referred to them as the "sons of thunder" *(Mark 3:17).*

▶ John is the only Biblical author who wrote two books containing only one chapter.

## BY THE NUMBERS

1
CHAPTER

13
VERSES

302
WORDS

# KEY PASSAGE

"And this is love: that we walk in obedience to his commands. As you have heard from the beginning, his command is that you walk in love" *(verse 6).*

# 3 JOHN

## DID YOU KNOW ?

▶ This letter from John contains only 14 verses and is the shortest book in the Bible.

## TO THE PEOPLE

Rather than speaking about general issues or doctrines, John directed this letter more to individuals and their small congregation. In the 14 verses of his letter, he used the word friend six times and the word church only three times.

## KEY PASSAGE

"It gave me great joy when some believers came and testified about your faithfulness to the truth, telling how you continue to walk in it. I have no greater joy than to hear that my children are walking in the truth" *(verses 3-4)*.

### *More to the Story*

John expressed his need to address many other matters, and he hoped to be able to meet with the believers and speak with them face to face *(verse 13)*.

### BY THE NUMBERS

1
CHAPTER

14
VERSES

323
WORDS

## Up and Down

John's third letter was written to commend two believers, Gaius and Demetrius, for their faithfulness, while chastising another, Diotrephes, for his errors.

# DID YOU **?** KNOW

# JUDE

▶ Jude included quotes from two historical documents that are not a part of the Bible:
Testament of Moses *(quoted in verse 9)*
First Book of Enoch *(quoted in verses 14–15)*

# KEY PASSAGE

**"But you, dear friends, by building yourselves up in your most holy faith and praying in the Holy Spirit, keep yourselves in God's love as you wait for the mercy of our Lord Jesus Christ to bring you to eternal life"** *(verses 20–21).*

## Name Dropper

Jude referenced several Biblical names and places, including Egypt, Sodom, Gomorrah, Moses, Cain, Balaam, Korah, Enoch, Adam and even the archangel Michael.

**BY THE NUMBERS**

1
CHAPTER

25
VERSES

624
WORDS

## In the Word

Jude passionately appealed to believers to beware of false prophets and deceivers. Jude reached back as far as "Enoch, the seventh from Adam" to evidence his concerns *(verse 14).*

# AUTHOR! AUTHOR!

**Jude, a brother to James, addressed his letter: "To those who have been called, who are loved in God the Father and kept for Jesus Christ"** *(verse 1).*

# JUDE IN REVIEW

 **WHO SAID IT?**

1. See, the Lord is coming with thousands upon thousands of his holy ones to judge everyone." Who does Jude quote?
A. Enoch
B. Moses
C. Ezekiel
D. Haggai

 **MINUTIAE & MISCELLANY**

2. What does Jude say he was compelled to write about?

 **TIME TRAVELER**

3. You are the cities that serve as an example of those who suffer the punishment of eternal fire. What are you?

# REVELATION IN REVIEW

 **TIME TRAVELER**

1. You are an Ephesian. What did Jesus hold against your church?

 **HOT SEAT**

2. My church has kept God's "command to endure patiently." Where do I live?
A. Sardis
B. Laodicea
C. Philadelphia
D. Thyatira

 **MINUTIAE & MISCELLANY**

3. To what did John compare the first voice he heard?

 **TIME TRAVELER**

4. You are one of the four living creatures John saw around the throne in heaven. How many wings do you have?
A. Four wings
B. Six wings
C. Eight wings
D. Ten wings

 **MINUTIAE & MISCELLANY**

5. Which horse had the rider who was given power to take peace from the earth?
A. The black one
B. The red one
C. The white one
D. The pale one

 **HOT SEAT**

6. I am John. What did I see happen when the seventh seal was opened?

 **MINUTIAE & MISCELLANY**

7. What happened when the fourth bowl was poured on the earth?
A. The moon shattered, and its pieces fell to earth.
B. The stars fell from the sky and burned people on earth.
C. The sun was allowed to scorch people with fire.
D. The earth burned from within.

 **HOT SEAT**

8. What has happened to me? All I did was try to harm the two weirdos who were prophesying. What did the two witnesses do to incinerate me?
A. Breathed fire
B. Shot arrows of fire
C. Threw hailstones of fire
D. Hurled swords of lightning

 **TIME TRAVELER**

9. You live in a nation that is described as a dwelling for demons. Where are you?

 **MINUTIAE & MISCELLANY**

10. What does John say fled from the presence of the one sitting on the great white throne?

 **HOT SEAT**

11. Wow! The new Jerusalem looks great! It's amazing! Hey, there's something written on the gates of the city. What could it be?

**MINUTIAE & MISCELLANY**

12. What gave the new Jerusalem its light?

## What's in a Name?

The word revelation is based on the word reveal, which is the purpose of this book, "to show [God's] servants what must soon take place" *(1:1)*.

# REVELATION

## AUTHOR! AUTHOR!

This book recounts a vision given to the apostle John, who wrote a total of five books of the New Testament.

### BY THE NUMBERS

22 CHAPTERS

404 VERSES

11,399 WORDS

### DID YOU KNOW?

▶ The vision given to John came while he was exiled on the island of Patmos *(1:9)*, during a time of great persecution of Christians.

## In the Word

The word come (or coming) appears seven times in the last chapter, which focuses on the future return of the Lord Jesus.

# KEY PASSAGE

"The revelation from Jesus Christ, which God gave him to show his servants what must soon take place. He made it known by sending his angel to his servant John, who testifies to everything he saw—that is, the word of God and the testimony of Jesus Christ. Blessed is the one who reads aloud the words of this prophecy, and blessed are those who hear it and take to heart what is written in it, because the time is near" *(1:1–3)*.